The Energi4U Program

Turning Your Chronic Condition into your Superpower in 60 days

Cindy Kosciuczyk, BS, MBA

AuthorHouse™
1663 Liberty Drive
Bloomington, IN 47403
www.authorhouse.com
Phone: 833-262-8899

Because of the dynamic nature of the Internet, any web addresses or links contained in this book may have changed since publication and may no longer be valid. The views expressed in this work are solely those of the author and do not necessarily reflect the views of the publisher, and the publisher hereby disclaims any responsibility for them.

Any people depicted in stock imagery provided by Getty Images are models, and such images are being used for illustrative purposes only.
Certain stock imagery © Getty Images.

"This program does not provide medical advice. This publication is designed to provide guidance and support and intended for informational purposes only. It is not a substitute for professional medical advice, diagnosis, or treatment. Never ignore professional medical advice in seeking treatment because of something you have read in this book. If you think you may have a medical emergency, immediately call your doctor, or dial 911. If you have medical or nutritional questions seek the advice of a qualified professional, as the author of this publication is neither a medical doctor nor a nutritionist."

This book is printed on acid-free paper.

ISBN: 978-1-6655-7270-5 (sc)
ISBN: 978-1-6655-7429-7 (hc)
ISBN: 978-1-6655-7271-2 (e)

Library of Congress Control Number: 2022918609

Print information available on the last page.

Published by AuthorHouse 10/21/2022

authorHOUSE®

Foreword by: Joseph Moore, MD
Sports Medicine Physician, Owner, and Medical Director, Pacific Wellness Center

Cindy has traveled the world searching and studying decades of individual health treatments, preventive therapies, and dietary strategies. Experience has taught her that looking for a cure for each individual symptom or diagnosis can be a shortsighted approach to healthy living. She found a better way and has developed an overarching approach to health. Her enduring quest for healing and understanding brought this book into reality. It is a must read for anyone wanting to take control of their mind & body and find the secret to their inner health.

DEDICATION

There are so many people in my journey of healing that have offered encouragement and support at the moments I needed it most. I would like to dedicate it to the most gifted healer I ever met: Dr. Anita Hunt Hickey.

Since her passing, I realized all the incredible lessons I learned about healing while collaborating with her. Anita was a provider truly dedicated to the healing arts. Besides having an encyclopedic knowledge of medicine, she taught self-healing practices and selflessly gave her time to her patients and all who knew her. May this book be a fine tribute.

CONTENTS

INTRODUCTION

"IF SOMEONE WISHES
FOR GOOD HEALTH,
ONE MUST FIRST ASK ONESELF IF
HE IS READY TO DO AWAY WITH
THE REASONS FOR HIS ILLNESS.
ONLY THEN IS IT POSSIBLE
TO HELP HIM."

~HIPPOCRATES

I grew up in a tight knit Polish American Community in Worcester, Massachusetts. My mother was a teacher of history and geography and many other things, my father a mechanical engineer with many patents in the paper industry. I have one older sister, Elisabeth. We were blessed to have our paternal grandmother live with us, and my maternal grandparents were an hour away. My father's father was a talented metal worker and his mother taught me to cook, sing, and sew. My mother's father was an accomplished entrepreneur, and her mother was a food manager at the Naval Hospital in the Boston area.

My family encouraged me as much as possible to learn, create, and dream. I have always loved languages. At home, besides Boston English, we spoke broken Polish. In New England, the popular language to learn is French. I took 4 years of French and I completed two years of Latin. There is the word, Sana. It means to heal, and that's what I originally named my 60-day program. Then I had to go back to the drawing board as I wanted to inspire many as to what is possible. I needed a unique title that conveys how my program would help. I loved Latin because I was a seashell collector and had labeled a whole collection by the Linnaeus Latin classification system. No goal was ever impossible! I thought about what my program did for me. I hope it will work for you and help you to achieve more energy. All of us who have chronic conditions wish for more energy to do even the most mundane tasks. That's where the inspiration for my title came from: Energi4U.

I skipped third grade because of my reading skills, and throughout my youth excelled. One of the first things that took place to bring me here to this study was to create a healing program for myself. Due to my mother's diagnosis of high blood pressure during my final years of high school, I began to study the suggestions the physician had provided for herbal combinations of food. No salt and less oil were prescribed for the dishes. I regularly helped with cooking for my family, and I worked in a pharmacy with the hopes of pursuing a career in chemistry.

I graduated from WPI with a degree in Biochemistry. In my junior year, I did a report with another chemist for a degree requirement. This study was designed to relate technology with society. "Pharmaceutical Dependence" explored the American public's desire for a pill to cure whatever, contrasted by ancient practices of healing with food and herbs. It lit the spark about healing for me. This would also be my first introduction to yoga to heal a back injury.

Right out of college I worked in the Nuclear Medicine Department at the University of Massachusetts Medical School. I was 21 years old when we published papers about our patient studies, and I was training techs in radio pharmacy. When my badge readings for radioactivity were extremely high because of the hours spent in research and operating the Radio pharmacy, it made me look at health in a new light. People experience fear at the thought of radiation. Understanding how it works is essential to managing it. Radiation is the transmission of energy as a particle or as a wave. If your body absorbs too much radiation, it can destroy your DNA strands, and the surrounding cells. It can also lead to cancer or even death. Practicing safety while in this environment is key. Badges register what quantity energy workers are exposed to, thus making it easy to monitor exposure while providing care. I didn't know then that working with dangerous chemicals would contribute to me developing an autoimmune disease. Because of my curious nature, I have worked in many fields since then, understanding that my whole career has had the elements of honor, privilege, and risk.

As a young child I experienced health challenges. I had surgery at 3 for a dermoid cyst growing into my brain. From that point onwards, my childhood adventures were accompanied with major ear, nose and throat infections and countless rounds of antibiotics. I developed an allergy to antibiotics, another reason for pursuing non-traditional solutions to my health issues.

My teen years were fraught with bullying and alienation from my classmates. Having skipped a grade and being always in the top 3 in class, annoyed my colleagues. I also participated in a range of activities in science, math, journalism, art and singing. This turbulent time created my ability to trust my own instincts and spend more time reading and writing.

In my twenties I married and moved to another state. My energy was directed at having my own art business and doing research for a small environmental firm. The relationship in hindsight had an element of control. If I became good at something, it would be time "as a couple" to move on to something else. We moved to Greece in 1988. It brought me an array of career experiences from teaching textiles to baking professionally. The beauty of it was that I had free time in the villages to learn nature's solutions to common ailments. I lived in Greece until I was 40. I didn't realize the herbs and habits I learned there would be an integral part of my method. This part of my journey gave me the tools I use to this day to govern my condition.

The reason for this book happened when I turned fifty. I was having all kinds of symptoms like face rashes, shingles, random fevers, and extreme allergies to medicine. It was a milestone year as I finished my MBA, got divorced and moved to Coronado, California. That year was one of the reasons that made me believe in what I do.

In 2010 I had iritis. Iritis is swelling and irritation in the iris of your eye. The iris is the colored ring around the eye's pupil. It is located on the front part of the uvea, which is the middle layer of the eye between the retina and the white of the eye. Uveitis occurs when any part of the uvea is swollen. Iritis (also called anterior uveitis) is the most common type of uveitis. Sometimes it's caused by underlying condition or genetics, but the cause is usually unknown. Most cases of iritis clear up with the use of steroid eye drops. If left untreated, iritis can lead to glaucoma or vision loss. My doctor, Steve Tayman, sent me to the Eye Emergency at Scripps. They did tests, found no damage to the eye, and sent me home with eye drops. Cost of the whole treatment? About one thousand dollars. Every time my eyes would flare up; I would put in the drops in about 10 to 14 days my eyes would heal. About a year later, wanting to renew my prescription I closely read the label and it said: Cortisone product, prolonged usage may eventually cause blindness!

I quickly called my Acupuncturist/Chinese herbalist and asked what she would suggest. I sent a friend to the store: two boxes of chrysanthemum tea and a jar of organic turmeric powder. I made poultices for my eyes with tea bags and warm water while drinking the concentrated tea as well. Each morning, I would add a heaping tablespoon of the turmeric in my coffee or tea to dissolve and drink until it was gone. My eyes healed in less than a week for a total cost of $8.00. My eye doctor suggested that I take an online test for lupus. I scored a nine out of 10. From here my journey to live a fabulous life concentrating on wellness began.

There are so many real-life horror stories of the consequences of an autoimmune condition. In my case, ignorance was bliss. Until the eye incident, I had believed that each of the symptoms were isolated. Looking back is always 20/20! One of the hidden factors was the stress of my first marriage that I never quite understood until writing this program. On one hand, it brought me to experiences I may have never experienced. On the other hand, it took me from my home. It was also a source of conflict because wherever I have landed, I easily made friends

and created a support network with that family of friends. Taking me away from all that I knew - happened without me realizing it. I came back to the USA under very dire circumstances and worked my way back up.

This is how I came to understand the most important thing in dealing with life's challenges is mindset. The practices I am sharing with you have over time integrated into my daily living.

I figured that is part of the reason as to why I did not realize what was going on as I kept my condition in a state of balance unconsciously. So come along with me on my journey with lupus. From finding what was wrong to looking into treatments and causes to creating a program that has kept me up and running.

With everything going on, it is unbelievable that I have had the energy for a demanding work schedule of 7 days a week for more than 4 years.

This was the result of going through the following in 2015: Publishing my first book, my contract at Naval Hospital not getting renewed, survived someone trying to extort money and threaten my life, having to give up my home of 10 years, 90% of my belongings, put my cat of almost 19 years down and moving to a part of town where I knew almost no one and having to find new work. In sales it took time to get back on solid ground. During this time, being well enough to work every day made me refine the methods that had been developing over time. I am asking you to try it for 60 days and see if you see some improvement.

1

CHAPTER

Creating Your Program

Have you been having issues with your health? Illnesses and experiences you cannot explain. Have you taken tests and different diet medications and it has not helped? Have they asked you for symptoms and no one could tell you what to do with them? Did they tell you nothing is wrong and that you are exaggerating or making it up? Or like me, have you powered through your illness. I am Polish from New England with the mindset of the only day you do not go to work is when you are dead. Some days the pain and swelling, fatigue is so unbearable that you wondered why bother? I would try to figure out what I could possibly do to make it through the day.

All these reasons are why I created this program. For years I had odd symptoms that I approached singularly. Oh, I have this rash on my face, I have worked as a baker for years so is it the extreme heat and cold that causes this. I am allergic to every antibiotic, guess that is because I took so many when I was an infant to toddler. You get the idea. For each symptom, the physicians recommended a cure to treat it. The time I had a sinus problem and ended up in the emergency room with convulsions because of the medicine prescribed. My quest for knowledge took me on a path to learn as much as possible with hopes of greater vitality.

Timeline:

- **1970's Learning to cook with herbs and exploring Asian Foods**

- **1980's Learning Yoga to work on a back injury**

- **1990's Learning the Mediterranean Diet**

- **2000's Exploring Ayurveda Food as Medicine**

- **2010's Mindfulness and Traditional Chinese Medicine**

- **2020' s the benefits of Physical Therapy**

No one put the pieces together until that event with my eye doctor. When they told me what was up, I investigated sites and data. Lupus Warriors and Lupus Support Groups. Exploring the fact that a portion of the sufferers did not do well with the heavy meds and practiced alternative healing methods. For years I have been assembling the pieces of my program together, later realizing that these methods combined have kept me up and running. Now I am honored to share it with you.

Let us Start with YOU! Take a little time to answer the following questions. If I am mentoring you in person, I would be asking you these questions in our first meeting.

Which of the following symptoms or signs do you experience? (Select all that apply)

- Frequent unexplained fatigue
- Unexplained weakness
- A recurring unexplained low-grade fever
- An unexplained loss of appetite
- Unexplained salt cravings
- Unexplained weight loss
- Unexplained weight gain
- An increased sensitivity to cold
- An increased sensitivity to heat
- Increased thirst
- Swollen glands or lymph nodes
- None of the above

Which of the following gastrointestinal and digestive symptoms do you experience? (Select all that apply)

- Extreme unexplained hunger
- Frequent bowel movements
- An urgent need for a bowel movement even when your bowel is empty
- Frequent unexplained constipation
- Frequent unexplained diarrhea
- Bowel movements containing blood or pus

- Rectal pain and/or bleeding
- Frequent abdominal pain and cramping
- Abdominal pain and cramping in the lower right side of the abdomen
- Frequent unexplained gas and bloating
- Frequent unexplained nausea and/or vomiting
- Frequent unexplained heartburn
- None of the above

Which of the following skin symptoms do you experience? (Select all that apply)

- Hyperpigmentation (darken of patches of skin)
- Frequent dry skin
- Frequent skin rashes
- Cracked skin that may bleed or itch
- Skin lesions that appear, or worsen, with sun exposure
- Patches of skin that are tight and hard
- A butterfly-shaped rash on the face that covers the cheeks and bridge of the nose
- Frequent ulcers
- A patchy loss of skin color
- A loss of color in mucous membranes that line the mouth and nose
- Red patches of skin covered with thick silvery scales
- A scaly scalp
- Unexplained hair loss
- Pitted, cracked, or crumbly nails
- Brittle nails
- None of the above

Which of the following vision or eye symptoms do you experience? (Select all that apply)

- Frequent dry eyes
- Dry eyes that burn, itch, or feel gritty as if there is sand in them
- Drooping of one or both eyelids
- Unexplained blurry vision

- Prolonged double vision
- A temporary partial loss of vision, normally in one eye at a time, with pain during eye movement
- None of the above

Which of the following muscle and joint symptoms do you experience? (Select all that apply)

- Tender, warm, and/or swollen joints
- Stiff and/or painful joints
- Joint stiffness that worsens in the morning or after inactivity
- Unexplained muscle weakness
- Unexplained muscle aches, tenderness, and/or stiffness
- Pain and swelling in the muscles, connective tissues, and/or joints
- None of the above

Which of the following urinary symptoms do you experience? (Select all that apply)

- Frequent urination (unexplained by issues such as prostate (men) or urinary tract infection)
- Tea-colored urine
- Foamy urine
- Bloody urine
- Pain in one or both sides of your back below the ribs
- None of the above

Which of the following mental and neurological symptoms do you experience? (Select all that apply)

- Frequent unexplained dizziness
- Frequent unexplained headaches
- Trouble concentrating
- Brain fog

- Confusion and/or memory loss
- Mood changes
- Irritability
- Insomnia
- Anxiety
- Depression
- None of the above

Which of the following sensory symptoms do you experience? (Select all that apply)

- Unexplained tremors
- Tingling or pain in parts of your body
- Electric-shock sensations that occur with certain neck movements
- Numbness or weakness in one or more limbs
- Fingers and toes that turn white or blue when exposed to cold or during stressful periods
- None of the above

Which of the following bodily symptoms do you experience? (Select all that apply)

- Unexplained swelling of your hands and feet
- An unexplained puffy face
- A frequent unexplained dry mouth
- Tongue enlargement
- Bulging eyes
- Unexplained hearing problems
- None of the above

Which of the following respiratory and cardiovascular symptoms do you experience? (Select all that apply)

- An unexplained rapid or irregular heartbeat
- Frequent unexplained shortness of breath
- Unexplained chest pain

- Persistent dry cough
- A cough that sometimes includes bloody phlegm
- Frequent unexplained sinus infections
- None of the above

Which of the following conditions do you have? (Select all that apply)

- Anemia
- Asthma
- Low bone density
- Hypertension (high blood pressure)
- Hypotension (low blood pressure)
- Hypoglycemia (low blood sugar)
- None of the above

By answering this assessment, it can help to organize where you need improvements and who you can ask for help.

2
CHAPTER

ENERGI4U
PROGRAM

Body Maintenance: Diet –
Movement - Herbal Remedies

My life has always been continually active. My career path has been full of physically demanding tasks. Lab work, chef work, oriental carpets, flooring and even a stretch at UPS on an airfield in the Houston area. Having lupus can make me exhausted and planning energy a bit interesting. I am of firm belief that work involving hours of lifting, may have really saved my health.

Body is the Way We Move

I remember so many popular sayings like: "**Your body is your temple**" and "**You are what you eat**." I know in my heart that this is true. Back in 2010, I found out I had lupus. I started reading so much information online. Most folks with this condition are on a full regiment of medications, and a small percentage regulated with diet and supplements. What totally made a difference was a video I saw that said: "What are you going to do, lay in bed, take meds the rest of your life? Why not get up and move?".

I became inspired by singer Toni Braxton, who opened about having lupus to the public. There are lists of autoimmune conditions, lupus being one that most people have at least heard of. Lupus is a chronic (long-term) disease that can cause inflammation and pain in any part of your body. It is an autoimmune disease, which means that your immune system — the body system that usually fights infections — attacks healthy tissue instead. It most commonly causes problems for joints, skin, kidneys, and heart, though there are some cases where the whole body is affected. The symptom most autoimmune conditions share is inflammation. Inflammation usually happens when your immune system is fighting an infection or an injury. Lupus can make your immune system attack healthy tissue; it can cause inflammation in lots of different body parts. Symptoms can include swelling and pain.

I am going to talk a little about Lupus as it's what I have learned the most about. There are four types: SLE (Systemic lupus erythematosus), Cutaneous lupus, Neonatal lupus, and Drug induced lupus. Experts also think it may develop in response to certain hormones and environmental triggers. An environmental trigger is something outside the body that can bring on symptoms of lupus — or make them worse. Lupus is not contagious—you cannot "catch" lupus or give it to someone else.

One of the most helpful events in dealing with my condition besides the impetus to move my body more, happened while commuting to work in the Gaslamp Quarter (a neighborhood in downtown San Diego, Ca.). At the time I took the ferry from Coronado (a neighborhood just over the Coronado Bridge and about 15 min from the Gaslamp quarter) and walked about a mile to work from the landing. One day I walked with my neighbors, an entrepreneurial couple and joined them at a technology coffee event. Juliet Oberding and her husband Terje shared with me a project that they were working on called Predictably Well.

It was an app that tracked how you were feeling, paired with environmental conditions like humidity that is a trigger for autoimmune conditions. A patent attorney that has Rheumatoid Arthritis, I trusted to share my information and was a part of one of their studies. It helped me to understand that flares are predictable. If you can keep a journal or use a fit bit or other tracking method to see what patterns your health has, you can mitigate their severity. For me, stress is my number one enemy, that with physical exhaustion, lack of sleep, eating foods that trigger the immune response and to some extent the weather can all adversely affect my health.

Recently, I have noticed that I start having a flare when I am more sensitive to harsh sounds and harsh words. I have come to be able to feel a flare coming on and do my best to lessen the impact. Simple behaviors like more rest, taking extra supplements, and doing positive things like yoga or taking extra time meditating to counteract how chaotic life can be. Let us explore together how you may be able to better manage your condition.

Mindset: Fixed vs Flexible

I signed up for CrossFit® for my birthday that year, 2013. Not knowing that this was the beginning of a long learning lesson. Learning ways to move with the heavy items being involved in my work was such a gift. A big thank you to Clint Russell, DPT and the folks at One Life Physical Therapy and CrossFit® Coronado. Their patience with working with me to change routines and focus on goals I can achieve. The other benefit of this unique combination is that if I do overwork an area, I go for a tune up for exercises to strengthen my weakness. What I read about and learned, having a coach to help figure a way to control and perfect self-talk. This potent mental skill resulted in my ability to formulate and achieve my goals—both inside the gym and out—with consistency and grace.

The natural extensions of the coach's habit of positive self-talk were optimistic energy. The mental toughness with this attitude helped to create an indomitable spirit clear in their physical accomplishments in the CrossFit workouts. I became inspired! A flexible mindset willing to improve was key to their success.

(Ref 2)

In fact, as I started planning the writing of this book, I met with my coach and asked him for key points about the importance of exercise in dealing with an autoimmune condition. The most important side he felt that helps is your mindset. If you have a fixed mindset, it's difficult to change. "It's always like this!" I can't do this!" A fixed mindset prevents individuals from developing skills, knowledge, and abilities to the extent they are capable of. The reason we do not achieve many of our dreams is that our mindset does not allow us to. Having an open mindset lets us live our dreams!

10 Key Characteristic of Fixed Mindset

The following are ten characteristics of individuals who have a fixed mindset:

1. **They strongly agree with these statements: "You have a certain amount of intelligence, and you can't do much to change it.," "You can only do so much to change how intelligent you are.", "People are born smart – or not."**
2. **They believe that their abilities (like intellect, talent) are simply fixed traits (unchangeable).**
3. **They refer to tasks as something that only they can do, and not someone else in their shoes could perform better at it than them.**
4. **They do not like challenges (as this will confirm their belief or hurt their ego) and they do not like having criticism when doing the task.**
5. **They are always focusing on the outcome of something or how well they do at it, rather than how hard they work towards achieving it.**
6. **Their behavior has substandard performance (not doing as good as people expect them to do).**
7. **They attribute their mistakes to their personality ("I'm just no good at this kind of thing.") rather than external factors ("This was harder than I thought, but if I could give myself more time and support,").**
8. **They are not fascinated with learning and improving for their own sake (for example, challenging themselves in a particular activity).**
9. **They are not interested in learning from their mistakes, but they often blame others for their shortcomings.**
10. **They believe that talent is more important than effort when trying to reach a goal or task of any kind. Most people fail in life because they do not see the connection between effort and rewards.**

"Developing a fixed mindset into a growth mindset can be done in several ways – the most important one is by realizing that you are the only one who can change your life." No one is going to come and give you an opportunity or take your hand when things seem tough. It's up to you if you want to do something about it.

CHANGING CERTAIN THOUGHTS INTO POSITIVE ONES Every time a negative thought comes to mind, try turning it around by replacing it with a more positive thought.

GET RID OF BAD HABITS, LIKE DOING THE SAME THING OVER AND OVER AGAIN!!!
If you keep making the same mistakes, chances are these will transform into something bigger and start holding you back from moving forward on a greater level. By getting rid of all your faulty tendencies, new opportunities will appear which otherwise wouldn't.

Let me share with you the advice I received from Suzette Miranda Owner/Manager/CEO at Life's Dreams (BS in Physiology and Holistic Nutrition, Prana Healing, and meditational counseling):

1. **We are each responsible for our experiences.**
2. **Every thought we think is creating our future.**
3. **Everyone is dealing with the damaging patterns of resentment, criticism, guilt, and self-hatred.**
4. **These are only Thoughts and Thoughts can be changed.**
5. **We need to release the past and forgive everyone.**
6. **Self-approval and self-acceptance in the now are the keys.**
7. **The point of power is always in the present moment. Believe!**

Happiness is Your Destiny. Here are Power Points that will become part of your "Belief System". Read these often. Memorize them so they become part of your Belief. You will then have a unique perspective on Life.

TAKE RISKS

It's the only way to achieve anything worthwhile in life. By taking chances and being willing to walk on a thin line, you will find out that there are unlimited possibilities out there waiting for you to discover them. (Ref 3)

Motion is the Lotion

Our body is a living machine. To keep things running smoothly, all parts must be working efficiently. MOTION IS LOTION. Or another term would be, movement is medicine. The benefits that simply moving your body can do and why it is crucial to your life!

When we talk about 'movement is medicine' or 'motion is lotion', people think, "Oh, exercise, yes, we're working our muscles." Right? The musculoskeletal system. The benefits of exercise go far beyond the musculoskeletal system.

Benefits of Exercise:

- **Aid joint lubrication and nourishment**
- **Improve flexibility & mobility**
- **Build muscular strength**
- **Help you sleep better**
- **Improve your balance**
- **Improve posture**
- **Ease joint pain and stiffness**
- **Improve or keep the density of your bones**
- **Improve overall health and fitness**

Movement can improve the ability to digest food. It can see decreased amounts of inflammation in blood markers and biochemical markers.

- **Improve food digestion**
- **Decreased inflammation**
- **More diverse gut microbiota**

Exercise improves the function of all our systems.

- **Increase exercise tolerance**
- **Reduction of body weight**
- **Reduction in blood pressure**
- **Reduction in bad cholesterol**
- **Increase in insulin sensitivity**

(Ref 4)

Circulation

The circulatory system's main function is to carry oxygen throughout the body.

This ensures that our muscles, tissues, and organs work properly. Proper blood circulation keeps the heart healthy – and that keeps the body alive. The body supplies signals that tell the heart how hard it needs to work. When we exercise, the heart must pump harder to provide muscles with oxygen to get us through a workout. I know some of this you have probably heard from health professionals, but the more we understand how our body works, the easier it is to fine tune our program.

Our circulatory system includes your arteries, pulmonary veins, and blood vessels. They take oxygenated blood from the heart and move it to the brain and the rest of the body. Then the deoxygenated blood, also known as venous blood, moves it to the heart which is like the body's engine. The right atrium part of the heart receives deoxygenated blood from an artery known as the superior vena cava. This arterial blood then goes to the right ventricle. The heart then sends out oxygenated blood through the left atrium and left ventricle and into the aorta. The reason I mention this, because in our discussion, my physical therapist was clear about the need for "Aerobic Exercise".

(Ref 5, 6,7)

Move it! PT makes it easy

A combination of range-of-motion, muscle-strengthening, and ambulation exercises are used to counter the effects of prolonged bed rest or immobilization. General conditioning exercises can help improve cardiovascular fitness (the ability of the heart, lungs, and blood vessels to deliver oxygen to working muscles), as well as keep or improve flexibility and muscle strength.

Physical therapy includes range-of-motion exercises, muscle-strengthening exercises, coordination, and balance exercises, walking exercises, general conditioning exercises. A physical therapist evaluates range. The therapist also decides whether restricted motion results from tight muscles or from tight ligaments and tendons. If tight ligaments or tendons are the cause, surgery might be recommended to be performed before progress can be made with range-of-motion exercises. Stretching is usually most effective and least painful when the patient's tissues are warm. Thus, therapists may apply heat first.

Three Types of Range-of-motion Exercises:

Active exercise: This type is for people who can exercise a muscle or joint without help. They must move their limbs themselves.

Active-assistive exercise: This type is for people who can move their muscles with a little help or who can move their joints but feel pain when they do. People move limbs themselves, but a therapist helps them do so, by hand or with bands or other equipment.

Passive exercise: This type is for people who cannot actively take part in exercise. With no effort from them. The therapist moves their limbs to prevent the permanent stiffening of muscles resulting from lack of movement.

Sustained moderate stretching is more effective than forceful stretching. There are distinct forms of exercise that increase muscle strength. All involve using progressively increased resistance. When a muscle is very weak, movement against gravity alone is sufficient. As muscle strength increases, resistance is gradually increased by using stretchy bands or weights. In this way, muscle size (mass) and strength are increased, and endurance improves.

One book Dr. Russell recommended was: The Supple Leopard by Dr. Kelly Starrett. It's a book that covers end to end mobility. The focus is on injury prevention by proper movement and perfecting our athletic performance. If you learn and apply it, you will understand how to move in any situation.

(Ref 8)

The Body is Water

One book that I read back in 2007, intrigued and made sense to me was by Masaru Emoto a Doctor of Alternative Medicine. Subsequently he was introduced to the concept of water in the US and Magnetic Resonance Analysis technology. Then his quest thus, began to discover the mystery of water. He undertook extensive research of water around the planet not so much as a scientific researcher, but more from the perspective of an original thinker. At length he realized that it was in the frozen crystal form that water showed us its true nature. He continues with this experimentation and has written a variety of well received books.

Dr. Emoto provided factual evidence that human vibrational energy, thoughts, words, ideas and even music affect the molecular structure of water. This very same water that includes over seventy percent of a mature human body and covers the same amount of the planet. Water is the very source of all life on this planet,

Its quality and integrity are vitally important to all forms of life. The body is very much like a sponge and is composed of trillions of chambers called cells that hold liquid. The quality of our life is directly connected to the quality of our water.

I have always felt better living close to the water, jumping into oceans and pools regardless of the temperature. In fact, while wintering on the island of Rhodes in the 1990's, I found winter swimming without a wetsuit to be invigorating. During my long walks, I watched as swimmers that were 70 to 80 years old jumped in for a daily swim in the chilly water. I tried it, I loved it and since then you can find me especially on New Years' Day going for a swim.

I had made a copy of the list of the positive words that made the water molecule the most beautiful. Prayers, a Buddhist chant, and other positive ideas. The words love and gratitude made the molecules align into beautiful snowflake designs. In a later section, I will discuss the benefits of chanting. It certainly made me feel more positive. Serendipity brings amazing lessons!

A few years ago, I had the extreme honor of being part of a multidisciplinary team in a Pain Medicine Clinic. Alternative treatments were discussed, and many contributed excellent results. We had a symposium with some of the most knowledgeable experts. Deepak Chopra was a speaker. I had posed the question about the importance of water. The discussion was about how each of us are made up of organic molecules that have been here for thousands of years. He also remarked that we are made of water and live on a water planet. He also has many programs and tools in place to bring meditation into the mainstream.

Deepak-Chopra-Mind-Body-Zone-Living-Outside-the-Box is a wonderful source of information. Living in San Diego, where he has a center, eases joining online workshops and area events. Truly inspiring, I purchased different books on meditation and mindfulness as unique gifts to some of my family! What is surprising about that is that they live in Texas and the focus on alternative methods is not as mainstream as in California.

Though I must admit I found my kind of folks the first time I lived there: As a vegetarian baker in a health and wellness restaurant that also had supplements available, and I house Naturopathic Doctor in residence! (Ref 9)

What do most autoimmune conditions have in common? Inflammation. What is the best way to keep the symptoms in check? Diet. There are so many plans on the market.

I suggest before making any drastic changes you consult your health practitioner. Best way to implement an addition or subtraction from your diet is starting with one thing at a time.

With autoimmune conditions, the most talked about symptom is inflammation. Inflammation is the result of your immune system's natural response. In normal functions this response fights toxic compounds, pathogens and cells that are damaged. This response affects your whole body including your brain. When this happens, the immune system stimulates the production of cells, such as white blood cells, and proteins to help eliminate the threat posed to the body's natural process. The white blood cells generated help to fight the threat. Very normal with injury, but the mechanism gone haywire is the sign of an autoimmune disease. Tests have been developed to measure this response, but many times it is difficult to detect.

Swelling is the typical symptom of inflammation. Chronic inflammation goes everywhere it can. It is known to affect the Endocrine system, the Nervous system, and even the Reproductive system. There is much research and literature discussing this response. General guidelines suggest eating an anti-inflammatory diet and avoiding as many processed foods as possible.

Lifestyle suggestions to keep inflammation in check include

Limit or avoid alcohol consumption, avoid a high fat diet, stop smoking, and do your best to avoid secondhand smoke. It's very important to get enough sleep.

Anti-inflammatory Diet

Bad Foods to avoid: White bread, tomatoes, eggplant, French fries, pastries, soda and red meat.

Vitamins to add: Vitamin A, D, E

Recommended Diet: Noom - See their site for an outline of an Anti-Inflammatory Diet with other information also a Mediterranean Diet is also a good plan.

Most autoimmune conditions have a great deal of pain and inflammation. There are different versions of this information, and I would like to mention the good foods versus the bad including a few extra vitamins outside of the Asian or Indian remedies. Here are some suggested additions to your diet.

Fatty Fish

Many seafood products are high in omega-3 fatty acids, which are known for reducing inflammation and helping an individual's body run more efficiently. Best types of fatty fish to go with are salmon, tuna, sardines, and mackerel. These are also great for helping individuals get their protein in for the day and they incorporate many different types of vitamins into their daily diet.

Dark Greens

Individuals fighting inflammation should consider throwing some dark, leafy greens in their next meal. Leafy greens contain vitamin E which helps greatly reduce inflammation throughout the body. Dark greens are also known for helping keep individual's upbeat and moving, reduce bloating, and overall maintain good health. Broccoli, collard greens, and cabbage make great side dishes, and are quite easy to incorporate into any meal, and spinach and kale are great additions to a salad. In general, leafy, dark greens have a lot more vitamins and nutrients than lighter greens, so individuals should make sure to add them to their shopping cart the next time they are in the produce aisle.

Nuts

Nuts are filled with antioxidants which help fuel the body. Antioxidants reduce inflammation and provide countless other health benefits as well, such as preventing disease and delaying the aging process. They are also high in fiber, helping individuals stay fuller longer. Almonds and cashews are the best bet, but any type will provide great health benefits.

Colorful Peppers

Colorful bell peppers have been shown to reduce inflammation for some individuals. Peppers are very low calorie and are filled with great nutrients, helping the body run efficiently. They also have high levels of antioxidants. Peppers can be easily incorporated into just about any meal.

Beans

Beans are high in fiber and protein making them an excellent addition to anyone's regular meal plan. One of the many health benefits of beans is their anti-inflammatory qualities. They also are filled with antioxidants and a variety of vitamins and nutrients, so, individuals should be sure to stock up next time they are in the grocery store. They can be used as a side dish, added to soups, chilis, and casseroles, paired with rice, or used in countless other recipes.

Ginger

Ginger root is best known for toning down inflammation. Ginger also helps ease an upset stomach, reduce heart issues, ease muscle soreness, and have many helpful vitamins and nutrients. Try drinking ginger tea by adding some finely chopped ginger to hot water. After a few minutes, strain out the ginger and enjoy! Ginger can also be incorporated into many recipes or use it as a garnish.

Tea

It is clear antioxidants are great for the body. They help keep things functioning like they are supposed to and keep individuals fueled so they are ready to face the day. Tea is known for containing antioxidants, as well as reducing the risk of cancer, and diabetes. There are a variety of types of teas, so it is almost guaranteed individuals can find something that works for them.

Fruits

Fruits are great for reducing inflammation. They are another food high in helpful antioxidants and will work well in keeping things running through an individual's system. It is very simple to incorporate fruits into one's meal plan. They make a great between-meal snack, keeping individuals full and fueling their body. They also are great in salads and work in a variety of breakfast foods, such as pancakes, muffins, or just thrown into cereal. Look for healthy recipes that incorporate fruit to start each morning right while getting in one of the recommended daily servings of fruits and vegetables.

Dark Chocolate

Yes, you can still eat healthy, while incorporating chocolate into your diet. When it comes to reducing inflammation, eating appropriate portions also helps reduce the chances of having heart issues and other health issues, such as strokes or diabetes. Dark chocolate can be eaten alone, making it a good choice for a midday snack. It can also be put into oatmeal, baked goods, or healthy homemade ice cream. Those feeling a little more adventurous can add some dark chocolate to their dinner meals, like chili, or put it into a spicy sauce.

Olive Oil

Olive oil is the foundation of the Mediterranean diet. It is considered one of the healthiest oils for cooking because it is mainly comprised of monounsaturated fatty acids, a healthier form of fat. It helps lower cholesterol and helps with blood sugar control and improve blood vessel function. In addition, the oil helps reduce the signs of inflammation in the body. It contains high levels of oleocanthal, an antioxidant that reduces the chemical markers of inflammation in the bloodstream, a sign of lower inflammation. Look for the Extra Virgin type - First Cold Pressed and check the bottle for the "Harvest Date'.

Avocados

Avocados have grown in popularity as a powerful health food. Although they are a fatty vegetable, they contain monounsaturated fats, the best type for heart health. Avocados are high in antioxidants, which we know can lower levels of inflammation in the body. Recent studies have suggested eating avocados can offset some of the inflammation caused by less healthy food choices. Subjects who ate a hamburger with a slice of avocado had lower inflammation marker levels than those who ate the hamburger alone! There is evidence indicating the large seed of the avocado may contain even stronger anti-inflammatory power than the rest of the vegetable. The seed extract may have properties like steroids and common nonsteroidal anti-inflammatory medications.

Mushrooms

Throughout the centuries, mushrooms have been part of the folk remedies of many cultures. These common fungi have complex chemical properties that are still being studied. The edible varieties have a high nutritional value, providing complex carbohydrates, minerals, and vitamins. As scientists continue to break down the many compounds in fungi, they are finding individual chemicals known to be anti-viral and anti-inflammatory. Among the anti-inflammatory compounds are phenols, antioxidants, and terpenoids. If patients are incorporating fungi into their diets for the anti-inflammatory effects, it is important they know the species they are eating, because only a few varieties are safely edible. In addition, the anti-inflammatory effects are greatest in raw mushrooms as opposed to cooked. I like some of the coffee products that include Reishi mushroom extracts, these are easy to find at Oriental Food Markets. I am also a fan of some Keto friendly coffee products like Trident which is local here in San Diego or Nootropic Coffee like Genius Coffee that boosts memory and brain power.

Turmeric

The compound that gives turmeric its color is curcumin, which also has anti-inflammatory properties. Curcumin has been found to work against the inflammation caused by arthritis, diabetes, and other chronic illnesses. Curcumin supplements are available that provide higher levels of this compound than the spice alone. It is also suggested that, in cooking, turmeric should be used in combination with black pepper. My first time learning about this spice was in 1998 when I worked in spice factory, Anatoli Spice in the island of Rhodes. So close to Turkey, the Middle Eastern Culture definitely had some influence. A compound in the pepper improves the absorption of curcumin by the body. The yellow spice turmeric is commonly used in the cuisines of Southeast Asia and the Middle East, it is also the source of the yellow color used to dye the traditional robes of Buddhist monks.

My Favorite Recipes

https://www.food.com/recipe/turmeric-rice-48162
https://theherbalacademy.com/perfect-cup-of-chai/
https://www.196flavors.com/horta/

Speaking of Buddhist monks, you may have noticed that I have many references to Asian healing practices. The approaches that make up traditional Chinese medicine (Such as acupuncture, tai chi, and herbal products) have been the subjects of many clinical studies and scientific reviews. When I was doing reading for a project way back in college, I had read about a restaurant in China where you went to the doctor first to diagnose what's wrong and go to the restaurant to have them cook what you need to eat. My last year living in Rhodes, I had read about Buddhist monks that would dive into the water and dry their robes with the power of thought. Sounds a bit crazy, but when I changed my mindset, I easily could swim in the chilling waters. So maybe they were on to something???

In 2000, I worked in an Asian import company and learned about home remedies, the Chinese pharmacy and where to buy ingredients. I later found and worked with three different acupuncture practitioners. One is a Chinese herbalist who's prescribed solutions have been a miracle in my maintenance of a state of wellbeing. Chinese herbal products have been studied for many medical problems, including stroke, heart disease, mental disorders, and respiratory diseases (such as bronchitis and the common cold), and a national survey showed that about one in five Americans use them.

I have been blessed to work on energy issues with a massage therapist / reiki healer. When involved in the Pain Medicine Clinic at Naval Hospital I was very blessed to work with a talented healer. Dr. Anita Hickey was a US Navy Captain, an Anesthesiologist, an Acupuncturist, a Pain physician, Reiki healer, and a master of Jin Shin Jyutsu. Jin Shin Jyutsu (JSJ) which is an ancient pressure point healing practice that was handed down from generation to generation. What is Jin Shin Jyutsu (JSJ)? The translation of JSJ is "The Art of the Creator through Compassionate Man". I have found some of their methods have helped me tremendously.

Acupuncture

Is a technique in which practitioners stimulate specific points on the body, usually by inserting thin needles through the skin? It is believed that acupuncture stimulates the release of the body's natural painkillers and affects areas in the brain involved in processing pain. Results from several studies, however, suggest acupuncture may help ease types of pain that are often chronic, such as low-back pain, neck pain, osteoarthritis/knee pain, and carpal tunnel syndrome. It also may help reduce the frequency of tension headaches and prevent migraines.

Tai chi

Described as a program of movement that combines certain postures, gentle movements, mental focus, breathing, and relaxation. Research findings suggest that practicing tai chi may improve balance and stability in older people and those with Parkinson's disease, reduce pain from knee osteoarthritis, help people cope with fibromyalgia and back pain, and promote quality of life and improve mood in people with heart failure. When I started my studies at Body – Mind College, we began learning basic Tai Chi as a method of movement to use when ministering massage.

TCM, (Traditional Chinese Medicine), was formed when there was nothing modernized in medical and biological fields, but there was something developed in Chinese philosophy, astronomy, and literature. Also at that time, people got a great number of experiences on how to deal with the disorders by natural methods, such as puncture, Qigong (mind controlling), and using the healing properties of plants.

Some talented healers in China began to summarize those phenomena and sublimated them to theory based on their philosophical and social knowledge at that time. TCM focuses on enhancing human body's resistance to diseases and prevention by improving the interconnections among self-controlled systems using different therapeutic methods, such as mind-spiritual methods (such as Qigong, Taiji boxing), natural methods (acupuncture, moxibustion, herbal medicine). These therapeutic methods are characterized by fewer side effects since they are natural. TCM evaluates the therapeutic results by comparing the symptoms before and after the treatment. The treatment is based on the differentiation of symptoms to clarify what is wrong in the self-controlled system.

TCM seeks the therapeutic mechanism from the human itself as integrity, and the integrity between human and its social and natural environment. The therapeutic mechanism can be achieved by activating systems, improving system connection, and enhancing human resistance. The mechanism in TCM is not like modern medicine that seeks the mechanism from cellular or molecular level (such as killing bacteria and viruses, an antagonistic method).

If someone lives well (no symptoms), she is healthy in TCM, whether she has some signs in cellular and molecular level such as high blood pressure. Many clinical studies have shown that combining modern drugs with herbal medicine would dominantly increase the effect.

For example, the effect rate in treating coronary heart disease with modern drugs (routine therapy) were 45.5%, while combining with herbal medicine it was up to 87.3%

"In caring for chronic conditions, sometimes standard treatments aren't always effective. Traditional Chinese Medicine, in many cases, has contributed to the cure, the relief of symptoms and great improvement in some patients".

Allyson Platt, L Ac.

Zen Shen Health Center

The important thing to remember:

Explore how to combine the two therapies. So let me be clear here that though I have use for Western Medicine in treating a specific symptom, I am more inclined to incorporate both the Traditional Chinese Medicine (TCM) and Ayurvedic practice to maintain a level of health. As I have mentioned before, the focus on cultivating wellness as opposed to focusing on disease.

CHAPTER

3

Meditation and Stress Relief

Arriving in San Diego in 2000 I figured I would study the healing arts, focusing on nutritional healing. When I first landed, feeling like a foreigner in my own country, I had thought I would return to Greece. I had to renew my papers and planned to attend a spiritual seminar. I did attend the seminar, and the few folks I met in my first weeks here were a catalyst to the amazing things that happen for me. I then decided to investigate programs of study.

There are unusual places to study healing here in San Diego, CA. You can take classes from Massage therapy, Chinese medicine, Reiki and the like. I took classes at Body Mind College. I was first introduced to this concept back in the early 80's with a class with the master himself, Jon Kabat-Zinn. I lived and breathed Donna Eden's "Energy Medicine" and Louise Hays "You Can Heal Your Life". I also started paying attention to what was going on physically and the connection to what was going on emotionally. Ref 11

Every system of the body is vulnerable to emotional discord as well as physical illness. The nervous system, an elaborate network of cells that facilitates communication between

our brains and the rest of our bodies, directly links our physical selves to our emotional life. Voluntary muscles, involuntary muscles, and our five senses can all be influenced by the emotional responses of our bodies. Stress can manifest a nearly infinite variety of physical responses that we might not be aware of. While these reactions can sometimes be adaptive and helpful signals (e.g., preparing for flight when in danger), they can also cause distress, leading to visits to doctors.

Using your Senses

The benefits of sensory experience are well documented. Our emotions and senses are tightly intertwined. Our different senses relate to emotions, psychologically and neurologically. If something looks or sounds or smells or tastes or feels nice, then we feel calm or happy. Thomson et. al (2010) defines this as a "Conceptual association." In other words, what we sense triggers a feeling. Research using functional brain imaging in human subjects has begun to reveal neural substrates by which sensory processing and attention can be modulated by the affective significance of stimuli. (Ref 12)

How we perceive and adapt to the world comes through our senses for our brains to interpret. We have five traditional senses known as taste, smell, touch, hearing, and sight. The stimuli from each sensing organ in the body are relayed to various parts of the brain through various pathways. Sensory information is transmitted from the peripheral nervous system to the central nervous system. A structure of the brain called the thalamus receives most sensory signals and passes them along to the appropriate area of the cerebral cortex to be processed.

Sensory information about smell, however, is sent directly to the olfactory bulb and not to the thalamus. Visual information is processed in the visual cortex of the occipital lobe and sound is processed in the auditory cortex of the temporal lobe. Smells are processed in the olfactory cortex of the temporal lobe, touch sensations are processed in the somatosensory cortex of the parietal lobe, and taste is processed in the gustatory cortex in the parietal lobe.

The limbic system is composed of a group of brain structures that play a vital role in perception, sensory interpretation, and motor function. The amygdala, for example, receives sensory signals from the thalamus and uses the information in the processing of emotions such as fear, anger, and pleasure. It also decides what memories are stored and where the memories are stored in the brain. The hippocampus is important in forming new memories and connecting emotions and senses, such as smell and sound, to memories. The hypothalamus helps regulate emotional responses elicited by sensory information through the release of hormones that act on the pituitary gland in response to stress. The olfactory cortex receives signals from the olfactory bulb for processing and finding odors. The limbic system structures take information perceived from the five senses, as well as other sensory information like temperature, balance, and pain to make sense of the world around us.

The sense of taste has been of particular interest to me as part of my career has been related to the food industry. Taste is the ability to detect chemicals in food, minerals, and dangerous substances such as poisons. Taste is a chemical sense perceived by specialized receptor cells that make up taste buds. Flavor is a fusion of multiple senses. To perceive flavor, the brain interprets not only gustatory (taste) stimuli, but also olfactory (smell) stimuli and tactile and thermal sensations. There are five basic tastes that get relayed to the brain: sweet, bitter, salty, sour and umami.

One the unique experiences for me was when I applied for a job at a place called Senomyx. They had us do a panel of tastings to see how correct our sense of taste was. I passed all the tests. The issue arose when we sampled an artificial sweetener. I had an adverse reaction which brought on a flare. Realizing that sensitivity to chemicals and my allergic reaction to most medicines made me understand that my immune system was set on high.

Receptors for each of our five basic tastes are in cells found in all areas of the tongue. The body is designed in a way that our sense of taste can distinguish harmful substances, usually bitter, from nutritious ones. People often mistake the flavor of food for the taste. The flavor of a particular food is a combination of the taste and smell as well as the texture and temperature. (Ref 13)

Aromatherapy

Aromatherapy is the use of essential oils from plants (flowers, herbs, or trees) as a complementary health approach. The essential oils are most often used by inhaling them or by applying a diluted form to the skin. Essential oils are used in aromatherapy such as lavender, tea tree, lemon, ginger, cedarwood, and bergamot. Aromatherapy is sometimes incorporated into massage therapy for various conditions, such as knee pain from osteoarthritis or pain, anxiety, and other symptoms in people with cancer. I first was introduced to the benefits of these oils, when going through a tough time.

I was living in Greece, owning a business, getting a divorce, and under incredible stress. A neighbor was an Aromatherapist from London. She made a specific blend for me and gave me suggestions for healing. I had an extremely hard fall in the market areas of Athens and was very bruised. The oils and massage helped me to quickly heal.

In 1998, I worked in an herb store in the Houston area and later that year on the production line in an herb company. As herbs seem to be a successful way to treat mild issues, and a good part of my program. As this is just a suggestion, I would like to share common remedies. (Ref 14)

Arnica: is considered a natural solution for muscle aches and soreness. What's more, research proves that "mountain tobacco," as it's also known, accelerates healing bruises.

Bergamot: With its bright, citrusy scent, bergamot, a hybrid of oranges and lemons is relied upon to reduce stress and uplift a negative mood. In addition, bergamot holds flavonoids that may organically support cholesterol levels.

Chamomile: Feeling irritable, and frustrated? Chamomile essential oil may be just the ticket. Thought to increase feelings of well-being and decrease nervous tension, it's used to relax—both at bedtime and when you're struck with menstrual cramps.

Cinnamon: Beloved for the cozy feeling is best used for an emotional lift, in that it soothes anxiety and promotes ease and comfort.

Clary Sage: Need to sharpen your mental skills for a meeting or presentation? This is your solution. Frequently used to bolster attention and improve memory.

Eucalyptus: If you're feeling congested, a key ingredient in Vicks, this mint-scented essential oil may loosen mucus and quiet a cough. Bonus points? Breath freshener.

Frankincense: Has more than one modern application. Studies have revealed that the oil may be helpful for those with arthritis, asthma, and psoriasis. What's more, the oil, with its fresh, woody scent, is believed to slow and deepen breathing and is commonly used in meditation. Also, to note Frankincense and Myrrh are the only essences when made into incense don't irritate the lungs.

Geranium: This pleasant, floral oil is typically used to reduce fluid retention, curtail cellulite and balance hormones.

Ginger: Fresh ginger, ginger tea, ginger ale—all are used to tackle tummy woes.

Grapefruit: Used to reduce jet lag and mental fatigue, the sweetly aromatic essential oil is also a popular ingredient in skincare.

Lavender: Used for promoting a good night's sleep, it's used for minor wounds such as bruises, cuts, scrapes, and sunburns, and relieve headache pain.

Lemon: A small study published by the National Institutes of Health found that expectant mothers who smelled lemon were less nauseous in the days to come than women who didn't. This citrusy essential oil is also used to fight fatigue and boost mental clarity. Additionally, lemon is perfect for your homemade cleaning products, in that it holds antiseptic and antibacterial properties.

Myrrh: Ancient Egyptians used Myrrh, along with linen and natron, to embalm the dead. The resin both perfumes and preserves the body of the deceased. The Ebers papyrus (a document written around 1500 BCE contains over 800 medicinal formulas, many of which are based on a mixture of honey and myrrh. The antimicrobial and antioxidant properties of both substances are now known to science. Myrrh gum was also used by the ancients to treat infection, bruises, skin conditions, and toothache.

Orange: Helps those suffering from anxiety and the exhaustion that comes with it and it may soothe the symptoms associated with PTSD.

Patchouli: The earthy essential oil is called upon to lessen depression, manage appetite, and aid with skin conditions.

Peppermint: Most commonly used for a burst of energy, this candy-cane scented oil is also used to elevate alertness and improve memory.

Rosemary: Rosemary is used to increase circulation and soften stress-related tension. It may be helpful in stimulating hair growth in those who suffer from the autoimmune condition, alopecia.

Sandalwood: Has an exotic aroma, it's derived from a tree that's deemed to be holy, and being the most expensive, is used for grounding, focusing, and balancing.

St. John's Wort: Its name comes from the fact it blooms on the birthday of St. John the Baptist. It has been used for depression and nervous disorders.

Tea Tree: with its other name of melaleuca has long been one of the most favored essential oils around. Functioning as a powerful antiseptic, it's used to calm insect stings and reduce mild to moderate acne.

Valerian: A grassland plant native to Europe and Asia, the roots have been used for thousands of years since Ancient Rome to aid insomnia. It has also been used to help with anxiety, sleep disorders, ADHD patients, nervousness, and trembling.

Vetiver: Relied upon in South Asia and West Africa, is used as a home remedy for burn relief, acne, wounds, and cuts. It's also used to improve overall body function, and, for those who live in tropical climates, to repel termites.

Ylang-Ylang: used to stimulate self-esteem and promote inner harmony.

(Ref 15)

One of my most memorable stories about aromatherapy has to do with tea tree oil. A friend was in Australia and brought me a bottle of the pure oil. I had heard about its antibiotic properties. Sometime in 2006 or so I was living near a canyon and would let my cat outside in the early morning.

One day he came back in with another cat and they were fighting. I grabbed a towel to grab the other cat and it bit me, down to the bone. It was 2 am and it was my right hand. I quickly flushed out the wound with water and figured it might be the best thing to apply. I poured half a bottle on it and made a tourniquet. I had a standard shift car, so driving wasn't possible. I had a prearranged walk with a friend early in the morning. They took me to emergency, got stitches, and for about two weeks I was concerned about rabies. Finally, I was able to find the owner of the cat. That deep puncture wound healed very quickly. I have worked in many roles in the food industry, and the direct application of lavender oil heals burns and bruises quickly.

I asked a colleague who specializes in aromatherapy blends for some suggestions for inflammation. She recommended some oils and blends that may be effective.

Single Oils: Myrrh, Wintergreen, Lavender, Basil, Eucalyptus
Blends: Valor (she loves Valor as it smells heavenly and phenomenal for emotions),
Pain Away (supports joint and muscle pain AKA Pain Away),
R.C. (supports respiratory system),
Breathe Again (opens airways and supports respiratory system),
Endo Flex (supports hormonal balance)

Nutritional Supplements from Young Living:
Thyromin (promotes a healthy and strong thyroid),
Sulfurzyme (hair, skin, nails, and joints),
Essentialzyme (promotes digestion),
MultiGreens (supports glandular, nervous, and circulatory systems),
Master Formula (full-spectrum, multi-nutrient supplement)

I would also suggest for individuals to look closely at their household and personal care items. As we discussed during our phone conversation, cleaners, candles, wax melts, laundry soap, personal care products, makeup, etc. can negatively impact our overall wellness drastically. It's called bioaccumulation or the accumulation of toxins within the body over a certain frame of time.

Natalie Moorman -Young Living Brand Partner #13300036
moorman.natalie@gmail.com

Ayurveda

The premise of Ayurveda is whole body healing which began 3000 years ago in India. Health and wellness depend on the balance between body, mind and spirit. In 1998 I went to live in Houston to be near my sister and her family. I worked as a vegetarian baker. My circle of friends at that time were mostly from the healing and spiritual worlds. A friend went to the Ayurvedic school of healing, and we exchanged ideas. Most importantly she gave me her cookbook to heal with food. I took a photocopy, and it changed my life.

I spoke with my trusted friend, John Riccio, and this is what he shared with me. "Lupus, in all its forms and effects, is a strong disorder that affects many people's lives all around the world. Speaking as an Ayurvedic Practitioner and holistic health professional, I only want to add some heartfelt words to my dear friend Cindy's great account of her life and times. Anyone can go online and search for "lupus and ayurveda" or "ayurvedic treatment for lupus" and find a myriad of results. This could be helpful in getting some basic information and new perspective for someone who lives with Lupus, but the key to understanding Ayurveda is beyond search results."

"Ayurveda is beyond the numbers, beyond the "facts" and beyond even the herbal protocols and holistic treatments one might receive when they go to an Ayurvedic clinic. Ayurveda is a science of love, compassion, forgiveness, and surrender. Without faith, yes faith, which corresponds with the first tissue of the body, plasma, one's foundation is weak; therefore, their strength, growth and integrity is at risk. Cindy's story shows how one's heart, will and faith can overcome the odds and lead oneself into joy, peace and harmony within their community and environment, and most importantly, within themselves."

He further added:" Many ancient texts, great spiritual leaders, and so forth have echoed the idea to "know thyself" or that the grand goal is to know God, through knowing the self. Ayurveda is *the* ancient life science of medical, practical, and clinical application. It is a vast ocean of scholarly knowledge from the pioneers of the pre-India Vedic culture. Its rich history is laden with experiential wisdom of vaidyas (physicians) who have stayed true to the "Great Three" texts of Charaka, Sushruta, and Vagbhata. I could go on and on about doshas, gunas, the Prakruti/Vikruti axis, Agni & Ama, the Shad Darshan, the Shad Rasa and the magical language that underlies it all, Sanskrit, but without proper education, chances are you would not understand a word of it.

All along the millenia, mostly unknown to the layman, Ayurveda contains (or exists parallel to - depending on who you ask) other grand sciences like Yoga, Jyotish, Marma, and Vastu shastras, which all individually could be studied for lifetimes each. There is a simple, hidden seed of pure, conscious awareness that mirrors the Divine, deep within Ayurveda."

"In my experience, people like Cindy, whether they consciously know it or not, exude and share this power. This power is humble. This power is innocent. This power is forgiving, and this power sees the Divine in everything. If one can see themselves in everything and everything in themself, where is the stress going to live? How is fear and pain and hatred welcome in this space? Does judgment have the energy to exist in this place beyond thought? Some readers might start to think now, "this does *not* sound very scientific at all!" Well, the issue then is not "science or *not* science" but that your thought of it, is in the way. That you are judging something you either know nothing about, know little about, or have little to know experience with firsthand."

"This brings us back to how Ayurveda goes beyond herbs and lifestyle protocols. It includes even the most amazing, thorough, and effective detoxification treatment that I have ever come across, Panchakarma (translated as the "five actions"). Without surrender to a higher power and an inner standing of one's place in the cosmos, there cannot be the type of healing and health that most of us all seek. Autoimmune diseases like Lupus have many root causes, but until there is a release of self-judgment and an open heart ripe for trust and compassion in and from the individual, how can there be a harmonious environment fit for a peaceful existence?

Surrender and an eagerness to heal are states of being that shine light on the last point of Ayurveda that I want to praise. The essence of living a life filled with ayurvedic practices is relationship. Understanding the nature of one's relationships is key to overall happiness, health, and equanimity. The nurturing of relationships is the heart of what is the experiential side of Ayurveda, the art of mindful living."

"Between one's eating habits and digestion, within one's work life, financial status, one's present, past & future, one's family and friends, and one's place within humans or the entire cosmos itself, everyone can use this divine guide to heal themselves from within. Healing one's karma and finding one's life purpose, in step with finding the peace with one's heart is also the type of art/lifework that heals disease or conditions like Lupus.

Lastly, speaking of relationships, the relationship between the client and their ayurvedic practitioner or physician (if you are so lucky to find someone so immensely qualified) is of a very profound importance. Due to the grandiose technical nature of Ayurveda, and the serious indications & contraindications of treatments, herbs, and protocols alike (not to mention the dense spiritual and philosophical dimensions found therein), it is nearly impossible for anyone to go at Ayurveda alone and find what they are looking for, or especially what they need. If this entry, or Cindy's book, calls you to investigate Ayurveda, please go to your local Ayurvedic wellness center or closest certified Ayurvedic practitioner for guidance. Do your due diligence in research and above all, approach your healing journey with love. All glory goes to God and the divine science of Ayurveda. Namaste."

- John V. Riccio, Certified Ayurvedic Practitioner & Lifestyle Consultant

John is a Certified Yoga Teacher, Clinical Hypnotist, & Holistic Life Coach, John graduated from The Ayurvedic Institute in 2019 after studying under its founder, Dr. Vasant Lad and staff. Dr. Lad was the leading pioneer of Ayurveda, bringing it to the West in the late 70's. He founded the Institute in

1984 in Albuquerque, New Mexico while still maintaining a clinic in his home of Pune, India. John has since continued teaching yoga and privately practicing ayurveda, while adding to his qualifications by attending The Southwest Institute of Healing Arts, for which he is nearly finished with its Integrative Healing Arts degree program.

Yoga

There are four historical eras of Yoga that will help us track a Yoga timeline. The first is the Pre-Classical Era. This form of Yoga originated 5,000 years ago in the northern region of India. It began as an oral philosophy taught by the Vedic priests, was to teach self-knowledge and internal wisdom. The historical Vedic tradition dates as far back as 1500 BC. The most famous work of this practice is called The Bhagavad Gita which you can find and read today. Patanjali is known as the "father of yoga," who offered a re-interpretation of yoga in an organized, written fashion. Patanjali wrote the Yoga Sutras, a collection of 196 Indian verses that displayed a theory and practice of yoga and compiled them into a "modern" text so that yoga could have a consistent message to its students. He organized a set of practices which he called "the eight limbs", a pathway toward self-knowledge and enlightenment.

"Many people think that yoga is just a stretchy form of exercise but is much more. Yoga teaches patients, compassion, and self-love. It teaches you how to focus and how to be present in the moment.

There are many types of yoga, Bikram, Ashtanga and Hatha, just to name a few. All are designed to help the student gain a better understanding of themselves through postures, mantras and or meditation.

After a few years of practicing balancing postures, I realized that the purpose was not just learning to balance but learning to focus. If your mind wanders, most often you will fall out of the pose. Also, in a challenging posture you are often told to breathe through the discomfort. This teaches the student to not give up and take deep breaths when faced which challenges in life.

Other than these mental benefits, yoga helps increase strength and flexibility. It also helps with digestion and elimination and helps create long lean muscles."

Erin Downey
Certified Yoga Instructor.

Post-Classical Era Yoga began when a radical set of people emerged declaring that there was a more comprehensive way to reach enlightenment. Yoga continued to develop and evolve in the east, the Mind and Body yoga practice.

Hatha Yoga, which eventually made its way to the western shores. Hatha Yoga came to the United States sometime in the 1930's. The first Hatha Yoga School was established in Mysore, India in the early 1920's. The program there featured medicinal practices (Ayurveda) that coincided with the philosophy of yoga.

A later development with B.K.S Iyengar, is known for customizing Hatha Yoga into a collection of 200 yoga poses accompanied by various styles of breath work to enhance healing in an individual. These components were designed to develop a strong, healthy mind, body, and spirit.

My first introduction to yoga was in the early 1980's, I had joined a class to work through some back injury. I began adding these stretches to my range of motion. In the late 90's, while owning the bakery "Cindy's Baking Cakes" in Athens, Greece. An American customer left me a bunch of paperbacks, one a picture book of Hatha Yoga. I began early in the morning for an hour to 2 hours to limber up. I was carrying 100 lb. bags of flour and the like and being in good flexibility and strength was key. When friends went to London, they got me a copy of B.K.S Iyengar, yoga for healing and I was transformed. I began to practice daily.

When I came to San Diego, I taught my neighbor some of these stretches. Finding the calming mindset just as helpful, I have continued to add some of these movements daily. I have practiced in a few of the studios around town, from Ashtanga Yoga, Hot Yoga and even Yoga and meditation class at the Chinese Buddhist Monastery. My quest for healing and understanding brought me to many paths and experiences. The mind is in control of the body. If you can find a practice that works for you, not only to help you work through the pain, but to help you achieve a state of peace. I find that staying calm lets me make the best decision for my condition. The beauty of Yoga is that you work at your own pace, and with time flexibility increases.

Chanting

Learn to chant, so that you may experience the sweetness of the work, for those who chant are filled with the Holy Spirit. – St. John Chrysostom

A **chant** is the iterative speaking, singing sounds, or words, often primarily on one or two main reciting tones. Chants may range from a simple syllable or melody involving a limited set of notes such as Great Responsories and Gregorian Chants. Chant may be considered speech, music, or a heightened or stylized form of speech. During the Middle Ages it got associated more with spiritual practice and prayer. Chanting may be a component of either personal or group practice.

Many faiths and cultures have their own version of chanting. Some of the oldest cultures like Vedic Chants, Bahai chants, Gregorian chants, Assyrian, and Native American are done in groups for a spiritual purpose. Tribal cultures like the Aboriginal tribes have a rich tradition of this practice. Most modern-day faiths have a unique version, like Roman Catholic psalms, Islam's Qur'an reading, Jewish Cantillation as well as the hymns found in most Christian faiths and Buddhist paths are versions of a chant including the Tibetan throat singing.

The concept of chanting certain mantras is of particular significance in many of the Indian and Hindu sects. The Hare Krishna movement is based especially on the Chanting the Sanskrit names of God. If I seem to go in depth here, it is because I have seen or participated in many of these traditions. As I write this, I fondly remember the Hare Krishna's on Friday nights in the Gaslamp chanting and dancing in their saffron robes, stunning tourists. I would smile as at the same time; the Jehovah's Witnesses would hand out cards asking if you have been saved on the same corners where bars would have staff milling about offering coupons for free drinks. I also was involved in some Eckankar groups, chanting Hu.

I first encountered chanting when in high school we took a field trip to St. Joseph's Abbey which is a Trappist monastery in Spencer, Massachusetts. It is known as a center of prayer and monastic work. Jams and beer produced by the monks are particularly popular. The monastery is also known as one of the origins of the centering prayer movement in the 1970. In the 90's I lived in Greece and Byzantine Chanting really made me feel the presence of the divine in my life.

Later, I encountered members of Eckankar, a philosophy that centers around the light and sound of God in all religions. They chant the word Hu. From the early 90's to the early 2000's this was part of my daily life. Hu is a word in many languages, mostly relating to the divine. Focused chanting helped me achieve impossible triumphs as a student of life, I have explored many practices, faiths, and philosophies, and know you must find what works for you. Trusting in your higher power/ God has been extremely successful for so many the world over.

As I mentioned previously, I kept seeing the chants of the Sokka Gai Buddhists in the most incredible places. I had someone take me to chant. As I write this, there will be the monthly chant at a nearby center. I have chanted Nam-Myoho-Renge- Kyo, the Lotus Sutra, for over 10 years. Buddhist teacher Daisaku Ikeda told students by Chanting Nam-Myoho-renge-kyo our lives will begin to change for the better once we put in the effort. This effort is fueled by faith and prayer.

Lately I do spend my spiritual life taking some classes at the Chabad, and as such services include a form of chanting prayer. What makes a chant different from a song? Three things: intention, repetition, and awareness. How can this help you? Find a word or phrases with deep spiritual meaning for you. Perhaps join a group of your faith to chant with. From my experience, faith is what makes a difference in dealing with life's burdens.

Music Therapy

Since my high school days, I have had friends in a band and experienced live music in so many styles. From rock to reggae, guitars to classical, music has always lifted me. Music can impact you by reducing loneliness, influencing your mood, and decreasing the intensity of chronic pain. When I injured my back because I fell and still had to pick up 100lb. bags of flour, I didn't know what to do. I called a friend who was involved in alternative healing methods, and they suggested I lay down on the cold marble floor and start singing until some of my staff came in and assisted in the daily bake. Singing took my mind off the intensity of the pain.

Turn up the radio. Sing a song. Lace up your dancing shoes or pick up a guitar. Making and enjoying music can stimulate your brain, trigger memories and emotions, connect you with other people and enrich your life, according to (GCBH), the Global Council on Brain health. "Music has powerful potential to improve your mental wellbeing and your brain health," says Sarah Lenz Lock, executive director of the council and senior vice president for policy at AARP. Music engages multiple parts of the brain — including those involved in thinking skills, movement, attention, memory, emotion, and language and helps them work together, according to the report, which is based on a review of scientific literature by independent experts.

Jacobo Mintzer, M.D., a professor of health studies at the Medical University of South Carolina says: **"When we listen to a tune that has a positive emotional context for us, it automatically brings up memories associated with it," he says. A song from your teenage years might remind you of your first slow dance, while another song might remind you of old friends. Even people with dementia respond to music from their past, the report says.**

Among the panel's recommendations:

- **Get up and dance.** It may be even better for your brain than other forms of exercise, at least one study suggests. If you dance with a partner, you get the added benefit of social connection and coordinating your moves with another person, Mintzer says: "You are really getting a full brain workout."
- **Listen to music when you exercise.** You will get a mental boost and extra motivation to keep moving your body.
- **Learn to play a musical instrument or take up singing, even if you've never done it before.** You'll gain a sense of mastery and boost your self-esteem, while helping your brain make new connections. (Playing an instrument throughout your life might lower your risk of dementia, some research suggests, but as the report notes, "we don't know whether performing music actually causes the brain to be more resilient to the disease.")
- **Consider performing music in public, with a group.** You will challenge yourself and create bonds with your fellow players or singers.
- **Enjoy familiar music that comforts you and evokes positive memories and associations.** But also listen to new music and let unfamiliar melodies stimulate your brain.

Art Therapy

I began drawing and painting around 3 or 4 years of age and haven't stopped. I first arrived in San Diego and worked with an art therapist as the vast differences between lifestyles and the trauma I had experienced for a few years were hard to express, with a combination of drawing what I was feeling and writing about it, especially poetry made a phenomenal difference in my emotional state. We will discuss journaling later.

Art therapy can be useful for patients suffering from chronic pain. Chronic pain is defined as a pain lasting longer than 3-6 months after the injury. Chronic pain has also been associated with higher rates of anxiety, depression, and anger. The cost of chronic pain can also put a financial burden on families, causing a further increase in stress.

Art therapy can also be useful for anyone experiencing stress. A statistically significant reduction of the level of the stress hormone cortisol was observed in healthy adults after just 45 minutes of doing art. Art therapy can be a way to channel one's emotions to produce something beautiful and heartfelt. Sometimes it can be difficult to put feelings into words that others can understand. Making art can be a way to help yourself and others understand what you are going through without the frustration of finding the right words to express yourself.

Art is not limited to drawing and painting. Other basic project ideas can include mask making, box making, visual poetry, card making, jewelry and beading, clay, crochet, and knitting, to name a few. We have seen that art therapy can simply be a channel for reducing stress and a way to relax at the end of a long day. For others, art therapy can be part of the treatment of chronic pain.

When I had the art gallery, I helped do a utility box painting project. The sense of purpose it gave me, and the artists involved was incredible. In 2010, chronic pain costs in the US were a staggering $635 billion. Art therapy as a non-invasive treatment can be part of the solution for reducing this the burden and is a mind-body therapy that recognizes the important ways in which psychological, emotional, and social factors can influence physical health.

Hydrotherapy

Hydrotherapy, also known as water or aquatic therapy, is a type of exercise you perform in a pool. The water should be warm, and the depth should be at a level somewhere between your waist and shoulders. Have you seen a water aerobics class in session at a recreation center? You've witnessed a type of hydrotherapy. A personal trainer or fitness instructor usually leads this kind of class. You can also do hydrotherapy under the supervision of a physical therapist. In this setting, you might use exercise equipment like a treadmill or stationary bike while in the pool. In addition to general fitness, people use hydrotherapy to improve circulation, promote relaxation, treat conditions involving the musculoskeletal system, ease anxiety, pain, and depression.

Like I mentioned before, I lived in Greece for 12 years. The best part was you can get to water easily. I embraced the local practice of winter swimming. A few years ago, there was a group that had weekly winter swims, I was so happy to join in. Here is the coast of the island of Rhodes. You can see how inviting the practice could be!

Pet Therapy

Pet therapy has a definition that includes animal-assisted therapy and other animal-assisted activities. Animal-assisted therapy is a growing field that uses dogs or other animals to help people recover from or better cope with health problems, such as heart disease, cancer, and mental health disorders.

Animal-assisted activities have the purpose of providing comfort and enjoyment for nursing home residents. A hospital's animal-assisted therapy program will bring an assistance dog and its handler to visit your hospital room. What it typically entails during a visit: they stay for 10 or 15 minutes. You're invited to pet the dog and ask the handler questions. After the visit, you realize you're smiling. And you feel a little less tired and a bit more optimistic. You can't wait to tell your family all about that charming canine. In fact, you're already looking forward to the dog's next visit. Animal-assisted therapy can significantly reduce pain, anxiety, depression, and fatigue in people with a range of health problems:

- **Children having dental procedures**
- **People receiving cancer treatment**
- **People in long-term care facilities**
- **People with cardiovascular diseases**

- **People with dementia**
- **Veterans with post-traumatic stress disorder**
- **People with anxiety**

And it's not only people with health problems who reap the benefits. Family members and friends who sit in on animal visits say they feel better, too. Pet therapy has been implemented into universities and community programs, to help people deal with anxiety and stress.

Pictured is my cat Trabelsi I had for almost 20 years!

Exercise:

Pick one new item from this chapter. At least consider adding it to your activities. At best, do some reading on the subject, and find a practitioner near you. Ask a few questions if you feel comfortable then please proceed. You might even meet new people with your same interests!

4
CHAPTER

Mentors, Coaches, Doctors

Mentors

What is a mentor?

A mentor is a person who can support, advise, and guide you. They typically take time to get to know you and the challenges you're facing, and then use your understanding and personal experience to help you improve. It's incredibly important to have someone in your life that you look up to and respect. This person becomes a positive role model that you emulate and learn from. Even more than a role model, this person can become a mentor. The purpose of a mentor is to help you grow as a person and become the best version of yourself. This may involve helping you achieve your personal or career goals, introducing you to new ways of thinking, challenging your limiting assumptions, sharing valuable life lessons and more.

Traits of a good mentor include:

- **Being a good listener**
- **Asking good questions**
- **Empathetic**
- **Encouraging**
- **Self-aware**
- **Personable**
- **Honest**

Who is a mentor?

Mentors come in many different forms, including teachers, friends, family members, and more. They take you under their wing to help you grow and develop. Here's why mentoring is so important, especially for children and younger adults. Mentors also provide their mentees with advice and guidance that helps them figure out what they want and how to achieve it.

Similarly, if there is something a mentee is curious about or unsure of, they can ask their mentor for advice on the matter. This can help keep mentees on the right path and avoid them making any critical mistakes by getting involved with things they don't understand. With a mentor, mentees can feel accepted, comfortable, and seen since their mentor offers a safe, judgment-free space.

Suggestion:

If you have somebody that you admire in mind to be your mentor, we recommend you reach out to them for a coffee, or a video call. Say you'd love to pick their brains about a certain topic and have some questions ready – don't ask them to be your mentor straight away! If you have good chemistry and you can see their experience being valuable to you in your career journey, then ask them if they'd be happy to meet more often and mentor you.

Leadership Mentors

One of the key tenets of leadership is the need to pass on the knowledge and experience to others. Most great leaders throughout history have made it a priority to grow and develop other leaders who can come in, take the reins, and lead more effectively. Mentors Motivate! They have high optimism and a love for life. Their energy is contagious. Mentors lead people to succeed through their own success and by encouraging others to believe they can also succeed. They set a pattern to follow. If you have good chemistry, and you see their experience being valuable to you in your career journey, then ask them if they'd be happy to meet and mentor you.

Spiritual Mentors

My life was changed by spiritual mentoring. I have always had a close relationship with God. When feeling that things are not going right, I usually double down on the prayer. If that doesn't work, I usually reach out to a spiritual mentor. During my high school years, we had a priest that was very active with the youth, the same while in college.

After my marriage, I drifted away and did not have much guidance. When I returned to the USA, I found a few different mentors over the years. Either close by or in contact by phone, zoom or email. Finding a mentor who exhibits unconditional love is key! As we wrestle with our conditions, at times we can be exasperating to our immediate circle of friends and family. This is a great time to reach out to a spiritual mentor.

Signs of a great spiritual mentor:

They spend time in prayer before meeting with you. They ask open-ended questions. Spiritual mentors are good listeners who share their own stories of how God worked in their lives in a powerful way. They support, encourage, and celebrate you. They may suggest some additional reading material to emphasize the topic they were helping with.

This year by way of work, I became part of a group that meets bi-weekly for a lesson, prayer, and sharing a meal. The group also meets weekly for a walk or hike in nature. I find having this spiritual support extremely beneficial.

The Challenger

If you want to grow, you will want some challengers in your life who will tell you when they think you're doing something wrong or if you need to spend more time thinking something through. They ask the tough questions that help you analyze your situation realistically. They don't sugarcoat and they'll honestly tell you if your idea is a bad one or if your plan is only half thought out. This criticism, if it comes from the right place, will help you get on the right path and avoid costly mistakes. My work environments include some challenger types. Their intention is to bring out my very best qualities. They have experience working with many employees and are intuitive about how good they can really be. It certainly can greatly improve your knowledge and self-awareness.

The Cheerleader

Having the positive support of a Cheerleader can give you the necessary motivation to keep going. Our parents, spouses and good friends can fill this role for us in many ways: and professionally, having a person in your field saying, "you can do this" can be a tremendous asset. A Cheerleader is someone who will be genuinely happy for you when you succeed and who will cheer you on when you might be struggling. I have some senior friends who are on the same intellectual level that make sharing new ideas easy and offer thoughtful guidance. My Saturday coffee group included a retired Navy Seal Captain, a retired Psychology Professor, and a Human Resources expert. Having their loving encouragement weekly has helped me persevere on the toughest of days.

The Coach

Coaches are there when you need someone to help you think through difficult problems. They are there for support and accountability. A good coach doesn't solve your problems for you; they help you see both the problem and your role a bit more clearly. They do this by observing, listening, asking focused questions, reflecting, and challenging. Coaches can suggest strategies for solving problems you might not have considered and can help you think "bigger picture" on ideas and possible solutions. One of my bosses has been involved in sports coaching for many years, and his words of guidance and support typically involve the mindset to approach problems. It's always refreshing to speak with coaches to learn a strategy for a difficult situation. Because the advice comes from an honest place of concern, it makes it easier to express the challenges you are facing.

The Connector

The Connector gets satisfaction from making connections. They willingly open about their personal or professional network to others. They are motivated by connecting people with one another to share ideas, passion, and energy. This type of mentor is an asset to both your personal and professional life. Sometimes it really is who you know that can make the difference! I have a mentor in the non-profit I belong to that always introduces me to inspiring people. I have a friend involved in politics that is happy to include me and invite me to gatherings that would be great for networking.

The Educator

An Educator is a person who takes the time to sit down and share their expertise with those who want to learn. Educators love to help others by sharing their wisdom. They want to see everyone succeed! I have a particular challenge at work with an aspect of my design work. The challenge of having to submit my work to a person with the highest of standards, sometimes creates a bit of stress and has a potential for errors. The person working with my data, spoke with me in a polite manner and offered to meet to review and show a different way to approach the task. I am feeling such gratitude.

The Idea Generator

Are you tapping into your creative side? Are you taking time to play? Sometimes we get lost in the day-to-day struggles and we forget to have fun. Play and fun are necessary to allow us to free our minds to look at the big picture. Is this the life we imagined? Can we adjust in either our personal or professional life? The Idea Generator takes on the role of "thought partner" and helps you to open your mind to new experiences and new opportunities.

The Librarian

As you navigate through life, it's helpful to be able to pull from various resources to help you get along. The Librarian has a wealth of information on your community, clubs, organizations, and support systems. In my writing in the rug world, it began with the encouragement of one such mentor, Barry O'Connell. He has a vast knowledge of the subject and stories to help make it fun and interesting. This type of mentor is so valuable as they know a resource for almost any need and are aware of where to go to get questions answered or to get things done. I have two friends that are librarians! What a blessing!

The Super Star

Find people who you admire. People who are living parts of their life in a way you aspire to, or who currently have the career that you want to have. Spend time with them and get to know their routines, their resources, how they go about their days. You can gain valuable insight into steps you might want to take to get you closer to your goals! I wrote and interacted with an entrepreneur group for two years. The amazing people I met and was inspired by got me through the worst of my days.

Lesson: focus on the tasks you can do instead of obsessing about the ones you cannot.

The Teammate

Some days you just need an awesome listener. Someone to remind you that it's okay and tomorrow is another day. A good teammate realizes that you aren't always looking for a solution to your problem, or a motivational speech to spur you on. You just need someone to listen with a sympathetic ear, and then allow you to move on. A truly great mentor often embodies more than one of these personality profiles. Look for mentors who know when to step in, when to push, when to teach, and when to inspire. Making these connections and having these relationships available to you means that you can pull from these resources whenever you might have the need.

Take a moment and reflect on what you might also have to offer to someone else. Be aware of the needs of others around you and step in if you are able. Mentoring can be a very rewarding experience for all involved! One of the most inspiring speeches I listen to when feeling overwhelmed is the speech of Admiral McRaven, the famous make your bed speech. I highly recommend it!

I had the honor of meeting Admiral McRaven, and it's a story I will never forget. As the program director of the Coronado Optimists for 7 years, finding and scheduling a weekly speaker at times had been challenging. One of my favorite mentors, who recently passed away, Admiral Irish Flynn, called me at the last minute to switch my speaker to Admiral McRaven with the stipulation that no media was involved. I had to reschedule a former NBC correspondent, Brad Willis. I told him that day that one of the Optimist's old Navy buddies was in town and they asked him to speak. Hearing a version of that speech really touched my soul. When we have challenges, think how getting through them will give you superpower! I also reflect on the fact that there are so many people in the world suffering and keeping a smiling face through the worst of things. You and I too can gather strength from adversity.

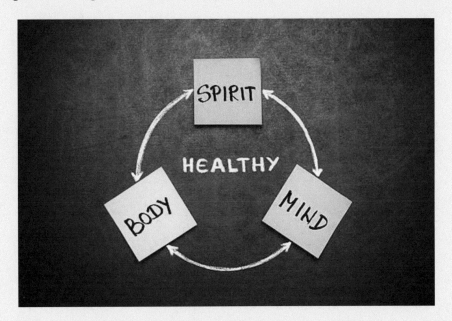

My most treasured mentors:

Captain Dan Hendrickson: He mentored me during best and worst of times, always giving valuable advice and humor.

Norma Lehman, Optimist: She taught me so many things of how to be an effective community leader and how important it is to inspire and encourage youth.

Barry O'Connell: Encouraged my writing and the importance of sharing it with others.

Damon Brown: Coached me through my first book and continues to share his wisdom of the entrepreneurial and writing disciplines.

Stephen Della Cruz: Taught me the lessons of mentors and the way to write consistently.

Matt: Since our paths connect because of both rugs and pain medicine, it encouraged both my writing and my quest for knowledge.

Wayne Strickland: Retired Fire Captain and Suicide Prevention Advocate: Answers his phone always and talked me through a few very dark moments.

Mary Laviolette: Taught the power of praying with intention.

There are many more in my circle who give from the heart with their gift of time and an ear to listen. I highly recommend you find a mentor or two!

Coaches

Who is a coach? A coach is someone who instructs and works with students or with adult clients to prepare them for anything from performing at their peak.

Career Coaches

This coach assesses their client's abilities and interests as related to a career path. They then find a suitable career for the client and equip them with the appropriate technical and interpersonal skills for that job.

Writing Coaches

I was fortunate enough to have met Author and TED Talk Authority Damon Brown. He coached me writing my first book, has become a trusted mentor, and assisted in my second book. The struggles of a writing career are best to work with an expert. A writing coach helps you to become the best writer you can be. With feedback you can depend on because of their years of writing experience. They can help find the best style and organization for your writing. This project is the result of a most opportune meeting with Ariela Wilcox, the Literary Agent who oversaw the writing of my book.

Self-improvement-Wellness coaches

This type of coach offers an entirely different type of service, in that they focus entirely on personal health and well-being. These coaches are responsible for ensuring their clients avoid high-risk behaviors, stay on track with a plan for becoming physically fit, and attain mental clarity and an overall positive attitude.

Spiritual- Metaphysical Coaches

I was contacted on LinkedIn by Coach Henry Quesada. I worked with him through some of my most difficult challenges emotionally. He shared the thought that the sacredness of our existence is an adventure of self-discovery that unfolds uniquely for everyone. Everything that happens in our life is meant for us to awaken to a greater truth of who and what we are. The ability to live with deep peace, love, and joy already exists within us as expressions of our essential nature.

As I have mentioned numerous times about the connection of our mental state and our wellness. I explored Louise Hays teaching that there is a metaphysical cause for each of our ailments. Before reaching for medication to cure my symptoms, I would first with some help get to a root cause for my "disease".

Exercise Coaches

In recreational or professional sports, to develop skills that will help a person achieve life and career goals. I have had the blessing of having many fitness folks in my circle of friends. Always willing to help fine tune exercises and motivate, the right coach can lead you to success.

Athletic coaches

This kind of coach prepare athletes of all types and skill levels for competition. Using training techniques and psychological motivation, athletic coaches assist students to meet their athletic goals and to keep them performing at their peak.

Doctors

Autoimmune disease occurs when the immune system attacks healthy organs and tissue in the body. In other words, the immune system can no longer tell the difference between healthy tissue and harmful substances such as bacteria, viruses, and other pathogens.

To us, this feels like the body no longer recognizes itself, and the cells no longer recognize what is healthy. Think about this for a moment. If one thinks negative, unloving thoughts about the body and oneself, how will the cells know not to similarly attack themselves?

- **Celiac disease**
- **Crohn's disease**
- **Diabetes (type 1)**
- **Fibromyalgia**
- **Food allergies**
- **Hashimoto's thyroiditis**
- **Inflammatory bowel disease**
- **Lupus**
- **Multiple sclerosis**
- **Pernicious anemia (severe lack of B12)**
- **Psoriasis**
- **Rheumatoid arthritis**
- **Scleroderma**
- **Vitiligo (a skin disorder)**

Examples of disorders also thought to be related to autoimmune conditions are autism, chronic fatigue syndrome, eating disorders, Lyme disease, and narcolepsy. Autoimmune symptoms often involve pain, fatigue, fever, and general lack of well-being; most are considered chronic and incurable. A perplexing aspect to auto-immune conditions is that most people show no outward signs that they are sick and appear perfectly healthy to their friends and loved ones. In fact, until someone is diagnosed, they are often told that the symptoms are "all in your head" or a result of anxiety. Unfortunately, many with autoimmune illness have been viewed as hypochondriacs.

The moment I decided to accept myself just as I was, something inside me shifted. I began to look at life from a more open, loving perspective. Within about a year, I was able to connect the dots that led to recovery. Accepting myself did not stop me from looking for answers—it allowed me to love myself and my life more fully, which led me to a recovery that felt miraculous and simple.

General Practitioner

A primary care physician is a specialist in family medicine, internal medicine or pediatrics who is a patient's first point of contact. Research has shown that people who live in states that have more primary care physicians have better health outcomes, including fewer deaths from cancer, heart disease, or stroke.

I was lucky to find a great physician by my office. A former Navy Physician, with an urgent care clinic always gives sound advice. Aware of my condition and extreme sensitivity to medicine, he prescribes when necessary and maintains my records of health. Referring out, if necessary, it's someone I know well and I trust. Personal care makes a difference, especially in the way the world is. "It's been shown that communities with more primary care physicians have fewer premature deaths."

The benefits of having a primary care physician include:

Continuity of care

When a doctor is a primary care physician, he or she is "responsible for providing a patient's comprehensive care," according to the American Academy of Family Physicians. Routine checkups with the same doctor build a relationship beneficial to the patient. Over time, the primary care physician develops a comprehensive snapshot of the patient's health which helps diagnose illnesses more accurately. A primary care physician also collaborates with other doctors and healthcare professionals, to keep track of any specialty care a patient receives.

Medication management

About 35 percent of Americans take at least one prescription drug. Of those who use prescription medication, they take four on average, according to research by Consumer Reports. Because different medications are often prescribed by different doctors, there's always a chance of side effects when the drugs interact with each other. A primary care physician can serve as gatekeeper by keeping track of all medications a patient takes, noting any changes in dosages or frequency that could cause negative side effects.

Many electronic medical record systems used in physician offices these days will automatically flag medication contraindications, prompting the doctor to review with the patient any side effects he or she may be having. The primary care physician can then recommend changes to the medications or consult with the prescribing doctors to better manage the patient's medication regimen.

Time savings

When a patient has an established relationship with a primary care doctor, issues that come up in between annual checkups can often be addressed quickly. "While it depends on the type of symptoms and how severe they are, there are a lot of times I can manage a patient's condition over the phone," Dr. Franco says. "The more familiar I am with a patient's history, the more effective I can be in deciding the best course of treatment. The patient appreciates the time savings this can create."

Prevention

The more a doctor is aware of your overall health, the more likely they will be able to identify health problems before they happen. Having your overall health profile enables the primary care physician to recommend tests that can determine your risk of developing certain diseases, such heart disease and cancer and diabetes. If you're at high risk, your primary care doctor can recommend lifestyle changes you may need to make to help lower that risk and prevent becoming sick.

Behavioral health

Comprehensive care under the scope of a primary care physician includes monitoring a patient's behavioral health. The current recommendation is to screen adults and children aged 12 for depression at primary care office visits. Each time a patient visits his or her primary care physician at Baptist Health, they will be asked if they are feeling depressed or anxious.

"One in four adults has depression and many are unaware they need medical treatment," Dr. Franco says. "Asking patients about their mental health is part of the collaborative care model that primary care physicians use. We work with psychologists and psychiatrists to help patients get the care they need to address their behavioral health."

I am excited to include vital pointers about behavior. This section was Contributed by one of my favorite mentors, Dr. John Sexton, Clinical & Prescribing Psychologist (USNA...USMC...Masters x 2... Ph.D... Navy Clinical Psychologist...3 years at USU School of Medicine/Walter Reed. He became the world's first Prescribing Psychologist...UCSD Psych Services...retired)

Cognitive Behavioral Therapy

Learn Cognitive Restructuring with occasional guidance by a psychologist or other mental health provider who specializes in Cognitive Behavioral Therapy.

Behavioral Therapy since no behavior occurs without a 'stimulus' (antecedent) or 'consequence'. An Antecedent causes Behavior. **A -> B**. Pavlov paired the ringing of a bell with food appearing for his dogs. The dogs would salivate when the bell would ring at odd times. If your workout clothes were placed in your vehicle's passenger seat, you'd more likely go for a workout. **B -> C**. Behavior only occurs because of a reward or punisher. An example of this is the data about weight loss bets. You would be helped immensely by reading about and practicing behavior modification.

Cognitive Restructuring

I. An emotion **only occurs** after a thought.
   a. Situations don't cause emotions. Thoughts about situations do.
   b. If the thought (cognition) Is accurate, the emotion that follows will be appropriate.
   c. If the thought is inaccurate, the emotion (and even the physical & behavioral responses) will be extreme.

II. **Cognitive Restructuring** is simply thinking more accurately.
   a. Accurate thoughts are based upon data.
      i. Think like a scientist, who concludes only after acquiring sufficient objective evidence.
      ii. Don't jump to a 'concussion'. One can change how they feel by changing how they think.
      iii. You will have fewer and less intense negative emotions as you train yourself to dispute inaccurate thoughts
      iv. A number can be used to quantify anything in life. Use accurate numbers in your thoughts.

     v.   Anything in the future can be given odds. Be like a Las Vegas odds maker, who gathers sufficient data to make the prediction as objective as possible.

  b. In making a big decision, do a 'Cost-Benefit Analysis'. List as many pros & cons as you can list for the simply worded issue. Do not censor your thoughts as you make the list. Then weigh each item on a scale from 1= not important, up to 10= very important. Add the columns. The column with the largest weight wins. A thoroughly done Cost-Benefit Analysis will mean that at no time in the future will you be correct in saying "I made a bad decision".

  c. Remember that anything that has happened is water under the bridge.

     i.   Deal with the 'current' stuff.

     ii. Focusing on the past will cause you to crash, like a driver who only stares at his rear-view mirror.

  d. Cognitive-Behavioral Techniques beat Prozac. The National Institute of Mental Health favors the use of Cognitive-Behavioral Techniques for mood problems. The scientific evidence reveals its superiority.

  e. Avoid making these common **Cognitive Distortions**.
Overgeneralizing involves words like "always", "never", "everybody", "nobody"; e.g. - "Everyone dislikes me" or "I always get the toughest assignment". Don't see things in the black or white extremes. Most of life is in the gray area. To avoid Overgeneralizing, quantify your thoughts.

1. **S & M Thinking.** We try to motivate or shame ourselves and others by using the words "**Should**" and "**Must**"; e.g. - "I should have tried harder". Similar terms are "have to" and "need to". Instead, use the phrase "It would be nice if _____".

2. **Mind Reading** often takes the form of believing others are thinking negatively about you, e.g. - "Since they yawned while I was talking, they think I'm boring". Others often become upset when we attribute a thought to them that they didn't have. Don't mind-read, ask.

3. **Catastrophizing** is predicting horrible outcomes, e.g. - "I'll be lonely for the rest of my life". Instead, make predictions based on objectively derived odds. I have been known to do this, a bit of it comes from letting the fear of outcome distract from living in the moment.

4. **Binocular Trick** is looking at others and ourselves through distorting lenses. We magnify faults by looking at them through the binoculars. Then we turn the binoculars around, looking from the large lenses down through the small lenses, shrinking the good traits.

5. **Labeling** is name-calling. We might label a person "loser", "coward", or "idiot". The person may have behaved like a _____, but he is many things, a son, a student, or worker, and possibly a brother. Label the behavior, not the person.

6. **Personalizing** is attributing something to yourself when it has little or no relationship to you. Personalizing also involves excessively comparing ourselves to others. "He is smarter…better looking…more successful". Remember, we all have strong and weak points.

7. **Filtering** is only seeing the negative details of something; not permitting the positive aspects to shine through. Shift your attention to the opposite of what you are thinking. Or do a coping technique like relaxation or problem solving.

8. **Awfulizing** We inaccurately rate the degree of awfulness with statements like "This is absolutely awful". It is better to think "This isn't awful, just inconvenient", or "_____ would have been more desirable". This is a common illness for people who feel stressed-out. Move from "I can't stand this" to "I don't like this situation, and I can do things to make it less troublesome". It can be quite helpful to say to yourself many times a day **"This is good enough"**.

III. Resources:
'Feeling Good' or *'The Feeling Good Handbook'* by David Burns, MD.
'Mind Over Mood' by D. Greenberger, Ph.D., and C. Padesky, Ph.D.
'Thoughts & Feelings: Taking Control of Your Moods and Your Life' by Mathew McKay, PhD., et al

Table 1

A ⟶	B ⟶
Activating Situation (Something seen/ heard/ remembered)	**B**elief or Thought (This is the critical component, because an inaccurate thought creates consequences that are extreme.)
C ⟶	D ⟶
Consequence (An <u>emotional</u>, physical & behavioral response.)	**D**isputing Questions (Use these questions to challenge your **B**eliefs.)

Table 2

Example:			
New acquaintance said he'd call, and he didn't.			What evidence do I have that my Belief is true?
	"He doesn't like me."	*sad*	What are the odds my Belief will occur?

	"He drove in bad weather, and probably was in a car accident."	anxious		How important will this be in a few years?
	"People are always lying."	angry		What is the worst possible outcome?
		also experienced: shaking. nausea. headache; concentration decline		Is there another possible explanation for this?
		increased: heart rate & respiration rate & muscle tension		Is this situation good enough?
				What would I tell a friend in a similar situation?

Table 3

(When upset, write whatever you are thinking in this column. It will slow the very common rapid thinking.)	(Then select from the list the type of Cognitive Distortion you made.)	(Finally, write an accurate thought, based on hard evidence or objectively based odds.)

example:
New acquaintance didn't call.

"He doesn't like me." ⟶ **Mind Reading**

"He has probably been in a car accident." ⟶ **Catastrophizing**

"People are always lying." ⟶ **Overgeneralizing**

What is a pain medicine doctor?

A pain medicine doctor specializes in diagnosing, treating, and managing pain and a range of painful disorders. A pain medicine doctor cares for the health needs of people with acute pain, cancer pain and chronic pain. Because pain is complex and covers a wide spectrum of conditions, pain medicine doctors specialize in both the physical and mental aspects of pain management.

A pain medicine doctor typically:

- Evaluates your medical history and any test results you have
- Performs a physical exam
- Evaluates your answers to pain questionnaires
- Orders and interprets laboratory tests, imaging exams, neurologic exams, and muscle and nerve studies.
- Diagnoses and treats herniated discs, spinal stenosis, fibromyalgia, sports injuries, cancer pain, headaches, diabetic neuropathy, and burn pain
- Prescribes medications
- Orders electrical stimulation therapy, cognitive-behavioral therapy, and counseling and physical therapy
- Performs therapeutic injections
- Refers you to an appropriate surgeon if necessary

A pain medicine doctor may also be known as a pain management doctor, or pain medicine physician.

Who should see a pain medicine doctor?

Most people see a pain medicine doctor when their primary care doctor refers them to one. Other doctors who may refer you to a pain medicine doctor include back surgeons, orthopedic surgeons, neurologists, rheumatologists, and cancer doctors (oncologists). Anyone with pain, especially chronic pain conditions or cancer pain, should consider consulting a pain doctor for a proper diagnosis and the most appropriate treatment options. However, a pain medicine doctor is not a surgeon. If you need surgery, a pain medicine doctor can refer you to an appropriate surgeon.

A pain medicine doctor treats conditions and diseases including:

- **Acute pain** including pain after an injury, surgery, or illness
- **Arthritis**
- **Back conditions**

- **Burn pain** including acute pain during healing and chronic pain that may persist after third-degree burns.
- **Cancer pain** including pain from growing tumors and cancer treatment
- **Headaches** including migraine headaches, and tension headaches
- **Muscle and connective tissue pain disorders**
- **Nerve Pain**
- **Sports injury pain** including sprains, strains, deep bruises, dislocations, and fractures.
- **Vascular disorders**

I speak a lot about this type of help because of the time I spent on a project in the Pain Medicine Department. The value of this training was incredible.

Exercise: Find a health professional you can trust. Whether it's a physician or even a nurse practitioner. The key is someone to discuss what is working and what is not working for you.

5
CHAPTER

ENERGI4U PROGRAM

Creating Change with Journaling and Gratitude Practice

Purpose of Journaling

One of the great things about journaling is there is no "wrong" way to do it. You can even have fun journaling. Journaling is all about dumping that stuff floating around in your head and then being able to walk away from it. By externalizing your thoughts and feelings through journaling, you tend to have less to "carry around" psychologically. Your brain will thank you. Journaling also gives you the unique ability to look back and see how much you have grown, both emotionally and spiritually.

Keeping a journal helps you create order when your world feels like it's in chaos. You get to know yourself by revealing your most private fears, thoughts, and feelings. Look at your writing time as personal relaxation time. It's a time when you can de-stress and wind down. Write in a place that's relaxing and soothing, maybe with a cup of tea. Look forward to your journaling time. And know that you're doing something good for your mind and body.

Journal therapy, also known as expressive writing, may improve aspects of your physical and mental health. One study in the Annals of Behavioral Medicine, for example, found that people who focused on emotions and reliving upsetting events during their journaling sessions, rather than processing the meaning of those events, reported worse outcomes than other groups in the study. Please know that if you try journaling and you don't feel like it's helping you, it's okay to stop. There are other ways to express what you are feeling.

How to journal

Try to write every day. Set aside a few minutes every day to write. This will help you to write in your journal regularly. Make it easy. I suggest always keeping a pen and paper handy. I have journals beginning back in the late 1990's when traveling. I would write my prayers, hopes, and even recipes. Then when you want to write down your thoughts, you can. You can also keep a journal on your smartphone.

What to write about

Write or draw whatever feels right. Your journal doesn't need to follow any certain structure. It's your own private place to discuss and create whatever you want to express your feelings. Let the words and ideas flow freely. Don't worry about spelling mistakes or what other people might think. Use your journal as you see fit. Don't feel that you must share your journal with anyone. If you do want to share some of your thoughts with trusted friends and loved ones, you could show them parts of your journal. We just were discussing the benefits of having mentors. I meet with mine regularly and when I saw this, I figured out I needed to share it!

Mentor Journaling

Write about the people that inspire you. They could be people that you know or people that you've never met but have helped you become a better person. In other words, you are writing to the people that are helping you become who you want to be. These are people that lift you higher. Do write about what inspired you, how you have taken those principles into your own life. This type of journaling gets you in touch with your "higher self" and helps to define your goals.

Unsent Letter Journaling

We all have things we would like to say to someone, but we aren't able to for various reasons. In "unsent letter" journaling, you write down what you would like to tell the person. It can be whatever you want since you aren't sending it anyway. You can tell someone how much you appreciate them, how angry they made you, or how you want or don't want to forgive them. Writing a letter to someone, even if you don't send it, can be a cathartic experience. It's also something to consider sharing with your therapist. This really helps when you have a difficult experience, or you have an emotional trigger. With Lupus, an emotional trigger can manifest itself in physical symptoms. Sometimes it's a person that makes you feel terrible, especially when people don't understand the challenges of a chronic condition. I was in a difficult marriage, and it became impossible to communicate.

I picked up a book about dealing with anger from the Buddhist perspective, and it was like a miracle! I shared messages written and it created healing so many times I wrote letters I didn't share but defining how I felt made me able to work through the difficult issues.

Visual Journaling

In art journaling, the journal is more focused on visual design than words. You can turn your words into artistic representations. As I referenced in my article on how to get started on journaling. Some created journals that combined art with words. I write poetry and draw and paint. I take these two together and combine a picture that represents what I am talking about.

Musical Journaling

Create your journaling through sound. You may be a trained musician, self-taught, or have never created your own music. Musical journaling can be helpful to you, no matter what your level of expertise. Tell your story through music. Drums, for example, express sadness, happiness or even anger. And you don't necessarily need training or need to spend money on them. You can turn anything into a drum.

I remember one Easter in Athens in a group of musicians we started singing and one person had a guitar then folks ran into the kitchen we tied pots and pans to the backs of chairs, and even had someone with spoons. What a lovely way to express yourself!

Stream-of-Consciousness Journaling

Stream-of-consciousness journaling is particularly helpful if you are critical of yourself or if you have perfectionistic tendencies. I find it easier to choose a blank paper and a favorite pen and start with the first words that come to mind. Write a story, share what aspects of your condition you are having a difficult time with, and you will see that? By sharing those thoughts, it becomes easier to manage them.

In this style of journaling, you start writing and just keep going. You write free of judgment. Even if your writing turns into a scrawl, keep going until you are ready to stop. Remind yourself that whatever you write is fine, no matter how grammatically incorrect, "out there," or indecipherable you think it is.

Intuition Journaling

When we are under stress, we tend to get out of touch with our intuition. Our intuitions are right nearly 100 percent of the time. You may find yourself "stuck" when you don't listen to your intuition. You may have been in an unhealthy relationship with gaslighting where you were told you were crazy, resulting in you not trusting your intuition. This is the time to reconnect with that gut feeling. In intuition journaling, you write down a question you would like answered. Then you respond as if your intuition is answering.

For example, you would write, "Is this relationship worth saving?" and by channeling your intuition you may get the response, "Life is short, it is time to move on." Journaling requires the application of the analytical, rational left side of the brain, while your left hemisphere is occupied, your right hemisphere is given the freedom to wander and play. Allowing your creativity to have a voice and expand can be cathartic and make a big difference in your daily well-being. One of the most impressive classes I ever took was called "Drawing from the right side of the brain", which taught technique from the book of the same title. It helped to free up creativity!

How journaling changed my life, imagine what it can do for you!

Journaling/expressive writing has been found to boost your mood, enhance your sense of well-being. Writing in a journal can reduce the stress before an important event. It has been known to improve your working memory. It has been especially effective with those who have PTSD (Post traumatic stress disorder).

It's hypothesized that writing works to enhance our mental health through guiding us towards confronting previously inhibited emotions. This is because it helps to reduce the stress from inhibition, helping us process difficult events. We are then free to compose a coherent narrative about our experiences, and possibly even through repeated exposure to the negative emotions associated with traumatic memories.

What-is-Going-Well Journaling

Is it a style of journaling, where you note what has gone well during your day? This could be done through bullet points or paragraphs. We tend to focus on what doesn't go well, so changing your focus can result in feeling less burdened. When you realize how many things have worked in your favor during the day, those not-so-great things tend to pale in comparison. I also like to create a weekly task list. As you know, when not feeling well things like doing laundry or even making your bed can be so overwhelming.

So, my solution is to have a clipboard (with graph paper of course!) to make lists of my tasks. Taking a highlighter and marking them completely brings with it a joy that is indescribable!

Gratitude Journaling

"Gratitude is not only the greatest of the virtues but the parent of all others." Cicero

When you are doing gratitude journaling, you can write down things in your life that you are thankful for, or things that make you happy or content. There is an exercise that some people use that consists of a once daily "write five things that I am thankful for," and others write in the morning and in the evening. Whatever way you choose to do it is totally okay. The purpose is not to minimize the challenges you are going through, but to help your brain refocus for a little while.

WRITE!

W – What do you want to write about?

Think about what is going on in your life, your current thoughts, and feelings, what you're striving towards or trying to avoid right now. Give it a name and put it all on paper.

R – Review or reflect on it. Take a few moments to be still, calm your breath, and focus. A little mindfulness or meditation could help in this step.

Begin with "I" statements like "I feel…", "I want…", and "I think…" Also, try to keep them in the present tense, with sentence stems like "Today…", "Right now…", or "In this moment…".

I – Investigate your thoughts and feelings through your writing. Just keep going!

If you feel you have run out of things to write or your mind starts to wander, take a moment to re-focus. This is another fantastic opportunity for mindfulness meditation! Read over what you have just written and continue.

T – Time yourself to ensure that you write for a certain amount of time.

As I write, I gave myself 3 hours of writing before work! Write down your start time and the projected end time based on your goal at the top of your page. Set a timer or alarm to go off when the time you have set is up. In fact, as you know with chronic conditions, we can be prone to catastrophize our feelings.

Thinking things like last time this happened, predispose our feelings to fear. I routinely set alarms on my phone for how long to write, when it's time to make coffee, take shower, or drive to work. I find by setting these timelines I am less likely to stress. And in chronic conditions stress amplifies any negative symptoms and feelings.

E – Exit strategically and with introspection. Read what you have written and take a moment to reflect on it. Take the time to sum up your takeaway in one or two sentences, starting with statements like: "As I read this, I notice…", "I'm aware of…", or "I feel…" If you have any action items or steps you would like to take next, write them down now.

One great piece of advice from the Literary Agent who oversaw the writing of the book was: just keep moving forward, work on the present chapter, don't go back OR forward to the other chapters. You can always add, delete, or change something at the time of the editing.

Experiencing gratitude

Luckily, applying gratitude specifically through writing can contribute to most of the general benefits of increasing gratitude, and the outcomes reported from gratitude journaling include:

- **Boosting your long-term well-being, encouraging exercise, reducing physical pain and symptoms, and increasing both length and quality of sleep.**
- **Increasing your optimism and, indirectly, your happiness and health. Reducing your symptoms of depression, for as long as you continue gratitude journaling.**
- **Helping you make progress toward your goals.**
- **Making you friendlier, more open, and more likely to engage in prosocial behaviors, which can enhance and expand your social support network.**

What to be thankful for?

When having a trying day a few things can turn that mood around. Focusing on what is going right as opposed to what is going wrong can shift your perspective. I message or call the friends in my network that radiate happiness, it is contagious! Then if not I watch funny animal videos. Of course, writing! For example, I work next to the commercial flooring rep. There are volumes of samples. The way they name them is very inspiring to me. I saw a text that said, "I speak in color" and it inspired me to write a poem I put in my book, Weaving Life.

<u>I Speak in Color, I think in Symbols</u>

I speak in color; I think in symbols. My vision guides my life!

Colors are my universe. Dreaming nomad dreams.

The universal language is woven.

The weaver is an artist.

Beautiful wishes and nature's wonders.

I see so clearly.

I speak in color; I think in symbols.

I hear your thoughts. I share your vision.

Expressing life's wonders.

Soul has a dream that words cannot easily describe.

Thinking in the symbols that all of humanity knows.

Seeing color as emotion and feeling.

Sensing the light and sound that together create a vision.

I speak in color; I think in symbols!

Gratitude is a verb and a very amazing habit.

Gratitude is from the Latin word gratis "pleasing, thankful". It is a feeling of appreciation felt by and/or similar positive response shown by the recipient of kindness, gifts, help, favors, or other types of generosity, to the giver of said gifts.

The experience of gratitude has historically been a focus of several of the religions of the world. It has also been a topic of interest to ancient, medieval, and modern philosophers. The study of gratitude began in the year 1998. This is when Martin Seligman introduced a new branch of psychology. Known as positive psychology, which focuses on reinforcing positive traits. The study of gratitude within psychology has included the understanding of the short-term experience of the emotion of gratitude. It focuses on the benefits of gratitude to those who do this practice. The study concluded that gratitude writing can work on the body and mind.

While not conclusive, practicing gratitude may help the brain react more sensitively to the experience of gratitude in the future, and therefore, may also improve mental health.

In Judaism, gratitude is an essential part of the act of worship and a part of every aspect of a worshiper's life. According to the Hebrew worldview, all things come from God and because of this, gratitude is extremely important to the followers of Judaism.

In Judaism there is also a major emphasis on gratitude for acts of human kindness and goodness. A Jew is to perform "Tikkun Olam", to create a better world with every action.

Gratitude has been said to mold and shape the entire Christian life. Martin Luther referred to gratitude as "The basic Christian attitude" and today it is still referred to as "the heart of the gospel. Islam encourages its followers to be grateful and express thanks to God in all circumstances.

Islamic teaching emphasizes the idea that those who are grateful will be rewarded with more. A traditional Islamic saying states that, "The first who will be summoned to paradise are those who have praised God in every circumstance".

In the Orthodox, Catholic, Lutheran, and Anglican churches, the most important rite is called the Eucharist; the name derives from the Greek word Eucharistic for thanksgiving. The Greek word, thank you, phonetically spelled, euharisto is used passionately in that language.

What to be grateful for?

I was reading an article called the 100 things to be grateful for and found many of my favorites! Your morning coffee, good hair days, the movie that makes you laugh, thank you notes.

Things like seeing the look on your child's face when they receive a present, a great hike to name a few. How you feel when lost in a good book! The list goes on.

You realize that the blessing is, according to my friend Alex Montoya, is focusing on what you do have, instead of obsessing about what you do not.

What happens when we are grateful?

There are basically three steps:

Recognition: when you realize it's all going to be okay. Seeing the glass half full instead of half empty seems to flip a switch in our brains. The moment when you realize there are friends and family that love you and there are worse situations in the world.

Acknowledgement: When you see the light at the end of the tunnel. It's the moment when you experience hope that it all will be okay. You feel that you finally came around the corner to a place where you can take the steps you may have been too fearful to take.

Appreciation: You finally understand and appreciate all those in your life who helped bring you to this place of hope. You tap into your own inner strength which helps you to make the necessary decisions for your health.

Being grateful can help our relationships. In work environments, managers who remember to say thank you to their employees find that the people who work for them will work harder. In a study of fundraisers, those who received a pep talk ahead of time from their managers did 50% better than those who worked in the same traditional way.

Lesson of this chapter:

Make a regular habit out of journaling. Keep your journal close by. Turn to your journal in moments of need. Make your journal a judgment-free zone. At times we experience judgment from our families, coworkers, partners, friends, and even people at the grocery store. It's a lot. Our journals shouldn't be another place where we feel judged. Write 5 things every day that you are grateful for. Remember to thank others for things that made a difference in your day!

Exercises:

Create habitual thoughts of gratitude! Write down 3-5 daily!
What if you said to yourself: "My life is a gift" all day long?
Or: "Every day is a surprise".

6
CHAPTER

Consciously Creating a Support Network

What is Community?

A community is described as a group of living things with commonality such values, religion, norms, customs, or identity. Communities may share a sense of place like a country, village, town, or neighborhood. They may be connected in virtual space through communication platforms. Community might be their roles in social realm such as family, home, work, government, society, or humanity at large. Communities are usually small relative to personal social ties, "community" may also refer to large group affiliations: national communities and organizations, international organizations, and online communities.

If you read any successful person's biography, there was always someone (usually many people) who helped and supported her or him along the way. One study found that participants with greater social involvement were less likely to experience heart-related complications. Social support systems affect us in many ways by providing a buffer to stress. They are a resource that enhances our coping (dare I say, our natural thriving) skills and they have also been linked to the actualization of healthy behaviors such as: increased fruit and vegetable consumption, exercise, and the cessation of smoking. So social support has the tendency to affect not only our physical health, but our mental health as well. For example, Vietnam veterans with strong support systems were 180% less likely to experience symptoms of PTSD than those with lower levels of support.

Social support, as defined in the research, is often described in two ways.

Structural: Having many different social groups that we are involved in ranging from social units such as our families, work colleagues, neighbors, friend groups, or organized groups.

Functional: The function within these groups such as the giving and receiving of emotional support, favors, and support in the form of logistics such as assisting with food, housing, childcare, or financially.

Life is full of many amazing moments. The reality of chronic conditions is that how we feel has fluctuations. We have great days when we are invincible and conquer the world. We have mediocre days, and we have incredibly tough days that try our bodies and our spirit. In the beginning of this book, I pointed out the importance of mindset. At our worst, if we can remember the optimism we felt on the phenomenal days, we can shift our thinking to handle the rough ones. Having a supportive community makes it bearable.

For me over the years, I have found the magical practice of volunteering. During the worst of my divorce challenges, I became involved in community art. I have been a member of Optimist

International since 2007. I found this group while fundraising for an art walk, Art Around Adams. I had walked the 3 miles of shops to find sponsors. I walked into a Tax Office. They had a banner with the creed hanging on the wall. I asked about the club and its purpose, friend of youth. I was asked to speak, sharing my story of how I got from Boston to Greece then to San Diego. I enlisted their help for children's art classes they willingly helped, and I have been a member ever since. In the photo is the local Vietnam Memorial. The director of the volunteers came to speak to my organization in 2015. I became inspired and began to volunteer.

What's important to state at the time I was in a very difficult situation, that I could not change. Focusing on community and helping others lifted me up. I have been in various positions with the group over the years. The main mission of this non-profit is childhood cancer and helping local youth. I am currently a director of the Optimists of Coronado. The group has over 100 members and many of them with impressive military careers, even a few in their 90's. We kept things going via Zoom and now again in person. Their strong example of how helping others can easily take the focus off your health challenge. In the photo above you can see a group of all ages whose focus is to assist the youth in their community, a common goal can unite a diverse group. I had asked a member who is deeply involved in many organizations to make a comment about the importance of community, and here is what he said.

"Community is tangible and intangible. It's places and buildings. Its shops and pubs. It's stores and markets, but it is also the support and safety you feel from the people you live with.

It's the sense that your neighbors will come to you when you're in need. It's the appreciation for the security that is provided by your local police officers and firefighters. It's confidence in your town's leadership. It's gratitude for your children's teachers and mentors and coaches. Community is loving where you live and loving who lives there with you." Chris Ellinger, Optimist.

I never thought I would be a writer. In fact, I went to Worcester Polytechnic Institute to study Chemistry so I wouldn't have to take all those English Literature classes! When I was working as a substitute teacher at the American Community School in Athens, I joined a group called the Writing Project. It was an effort to get all different departments to add a written element to their curriculum. I first wrote some poetry in high school. For fun I worked translating spiritual poetry I loved into Greek. I was fascinated by Rumi and had a book I took around the world, Stranger by the River. I felt that others needed to hear their words.

Currently I belong to a writing group, the Coronado Scribes as well as the San Diego Journal Association and write for Bizcatalyst360, and Beyond the Bridge. Their input on my writing made such a remarkable difference, not only in the quality of my written word, but being part of a community that also wrote about life's tragedies and triumphs.

Through my educational years I have been involved in creative circles. Singing in choirs, creating scenery for plays, taking piano, language, dance, and painting classes. Taking a class is an easy way to create community.

Folks of a more spiritual nature may find their church community to offer the most strength and support. From back in the late 1990's I belonged to a spiritual group Eckankar. One of their main views is that dreams touch every level of our life. They may let us glimpse the future, or give suggestions for healing, or share insights into our relationships. Above all, they can and will steer us more directly toward God. I traveled a lot back then and everywhere I went I would look up the local chapter and quickly make friends and have some social support. I had become acquainted with the groups in Athens, Rhodes, Italy, Holland, Texas, San Francisco, Las Vegas, Canada, Massachusetts, and San Diego. It made a difference in the experience of being somewhere new. That might not be your style but finding people that you have things in common with can make your condition easier to transcend.

Human beings by nature are community creatures.

Finding places where we have a sense of belonging becomes more important and at times more difficult as we age. Adding a chronic condition can make it even more challenging. A good day or a bad day can be greatly improved if we know we are not alone. We as human beings are interdependent. The third level of Maslow's Hierarchy of Needs is "a sense of belonging and love." We have a psychological need for intimate relationships and, for many of us, we depend on those relationships to meet our physiological needs.

Now as of writing this I am not in an intimate relationship. At times it's discouraging when I open about it, it sends many people running the other way. The hard part is most of the time I don't look sick. I focus on being well so much that when I am having a rough day, it surprises some and many are extremely tough on me saying don't make excuses. It has really helped me to develop inner strength and find people and places where I am accepted and feel welcomed.

My condition was hidden in stories I made up in my head, like "You should be over this," or "You can't tell anyone about that part – it is just too bad (or gross or weird)," and the one that really kept me in pain, "No one has ever experienced what you are experiencing, so don't share because they'll think you're crazy." The key to healing is finding a safe space to share these dark feelings allows freedom and release. Just to have someone hear your truth is healing. It reminds me of this quote: "Community is a healing gift we give ourselves when we allow others to say, 'me too.'"

The common statement: But you don't look sick! Was best described with the "Spoon Theory". It's the statement that is used to describe the amount of mental or physical energy a person has available for daily activities and tasks, and I found it really applied to me. It was developed by Christine Miserandino in 2003 to express how it felt to live with having lupus. The visual representation with spoons being of units of energy that a person might have available. It explains and how having Lupus forces her to plan out her days and actions in advance, so as not to run out of energy, or spoons, before the end of the day. That is a big reason why I called my program Energi4U. It has since been applied to other phenomena, such as other disabilities, marginalization, mental health issues, and other factors that might place an extra – often unseen – burden on some individuals.

Christine Miserandino's

SPOON THEORY

You have 12 spoons to get through the day.

Take away a spoon if you slept poorly the night before, missed a meal or skipped meds.

Get out of bed

Get dressed

Watch TV

Shower

Read

Use the internet

Socialise

Make a meal

Light housework

Visit the doctor

Exercise

Go to school or work

#THIS IS M.E.

#endthestigma
@ukthisisme
thisismeuk.com

During the pandemic, meeting in person became difficult. The power of technology saved many people from isolation. Zoom calls became the connector to the communities and families. I have found that so many of the groups I belonged to online saved my sanity, and I suggest that if you don't have groups you belong to there are a few ways to develop this connection. On Facebook and Instagram, Meetup, find others with your same health challenge, hobby, line of work, or even family or cultural type.

For example, I belong to the Lupus Warriors, Facebook Poetry Society, Women of WPI, San Diego Business Network, and many groups in my passion/hobby of rugs like The Rug Room and What's my Rug, and even some national and international groups of enthusiasts. I found out humor really can turn the day around and made some friends like Virus Social Distance group, or Funny pet videos. Pandemic groups saved my soul: IBC, The Quarantine Network, The Quarantine Kitchen, for example. Sharing what you know can begin long term benefits.

The belief that no one in the world understands what we are going through or would want to be a part of what we are experiencing is a lie that keeps us from healing. When we are in community, that lie is broken, and light forces its way into the dark, freeing us from isolation. This happens by sharing, being seen, and allowing others to share and be seen. In that process, we often learn that others are going through very similar experiences – and they desire healing from it too.

I shared the fact that I was writing this book with friends from college. My amazement that one deals with Lupus, another rheumatoid arthritis, and another is in remission from cancer. Finding people, you can share your pain and your happiness with is a game changer.

We lift each other up when we care for our community

Perhaps I am in more groups than most, I just wanted you to know that there are people you can count on. If you are a spiritual person, most places of worship have events and support services in your area. Also, neighbors can be helpful. Many years I lived in a neighborhood and an apartment community where everyone enjoyed gathering for potlucks, birthdays, and such. Families can be far away or not able to help and it's a wise idea to know those around you if something serious might occur.

Being open about what you need and what you can help with can easily make lifelong friendships. One study found people who reported giving support (not receiving it) experienced even more positive results in their lives. And ironically, those who reported giving more support ended up receiving more support.

In a study of one support group, it was found that some of the group members experienced negative health effects, even with the self-reported positive social support and less anxiety. The researchers speculated that it was because the participants did not allow themselves to fully feel their negative emotions. To me the best thing you can do for yourself be authentic to yourself, to what you're feeling. Be honest about where you are at.

One wonderful surprise has been the support I have received from the medical people in my life who tirelessly answer questions, encourage and support even though they may have more than a full plate of life. "Stronger together" is an active verb. Find the folks that can be part of your team. I have been surprised by what I thought would heal me and what has really healed me.

One lesson I have learned repeatedly is how quickly healing progresses when I bring others around me and share my truth. It often feels comfortable when you're in pain or experiencing something hard to isolate and withdraw, to not expose your "weakness" to others, but I believe you'll find when you do connect, the most profound healing and growth happens.

Creating a community

Here are six ways to shift your thinking to community care, considering the needs of your family members, friends, co-workers, neighbors, group members, and others you interact with on a regular basis.

1. **Empathize**
2. **Check in Regularly**
3. **Prioritize Rest**
4. **Offer help that you can do**
5. **Intervene when they can't help themselves**
6. **Socialize**

Please keep an open mind out for opportunities you come across to learn more about being human and the capacity for healing. As individuals, we must be aware every moment of the day of how we feel and what we need to do to maintain this balance. Our awareness of ourselves, others and external conditions give us an insight that most don't experience.

I am grateful you joined me on this journey from illness to wellness, making the best of our condition, and creating the life you want and deserve! Please contact me if you wish for a personal mentor as you set a new foundation of wellness, creativity, and love in your life. I invite you to join me in looking at your condition as your superpower. Thank you!

I really recommend this as though it might be difficult to change your situation. There are others who would greatly benefit from your help no matter how small or large the effort.

TURNING YOUR CHRONIC CONDITION TO YOUR SUPERPOWER WITH ENERGI4U

Module 1: (or Week 1)

Take the quiz in chapter one to help pinpoint your common health challenges. If you do not have a health practitioner at this time, I challenge you to make an appointment with one you would feel comfortable with.

Module 2:

Add one activity a week to your schedule: whether it's walking, yoga, stretching etc. If not moving well, investigate seeing a Physical Therapist or Chiropractor.

Module 3:

Add a new food or supplement to your routine and eliminate one habit that may be jeopardizing your health.

Module 4:

Call or write someone from your past that greatly influenced your life in a positive way. Find something you would like to learn more about and contact someone who can help you to achieve this.

Module 5:

Gratitude exercise. For the next ten days write at least one thing and one person you are thankful for. After ten days, choose one to call or write to.

Module 6:

Journaling exercise. Write one page every day. Half with things you feel unhappy or stressed about, and the other possible solutions

Module 7:

Find a meditation practice that suits you and try 5 minutes a day. If you can, add 5 minutes when you first wake up and 5 at the end of the day.

Module 8:

Investigate community groups either in person or online and join one.

Module 9:

Make a commitment to do one volunteer activity (read children a story, make a weekly call to a family member who is alone, and if health permits, do something like a donation to a shelter or to a group that ministers to the disadvantaged).

Remember that there are others who would greatly benefit from your help no matter how small or large the effort.

EPILOGUE

I would like to thank you for coming on this journey with me. I would love to hear from you if it helped in any way or if you have brilliant ideas to add. Thank you!

The idea for this book began a few years ago. I started to focus more on the natural ways to heal back in the 1990's. Writing this book was way more phenomenal than I had imagined. When sharing my health evolution, I remembered bits of knowledge I had discovered, but forgot. Like any healthy behavior, making changes takes serious commitment as well as the willingness to get back on track when we pause.

I have worked in hospitals and as such know that Western medicine has many excellent solutions for healing, at the same time knowing that "alternative medicine" at times has an even better one. I had thought that the information I have been collecting was common to most, and in speaking with friends, colleagues, and health professionals, that my story may be of help to others.

ACKNOWLEDGEMENTS

There are so many to thank. Mentors, friends, family, and coaches who navigated with me through good times and the bad. Thank you for believing in me. Special thanks to **Ariela Wilcox** who believed this information should be public.

Sincere thanks to all my angel friends who contributed to making this a reality: **Clint Russell DPT, Dr. Joe Moore, Dr. John Sexton, Chuck Hardwick, Juliet Oberding, Suzette Miranda, Allyson Platt, LAC, HHP, John V. Riccio, Christian Ellinger, Tanja van Tooren Pijapaert, Wayne Strickland, Kristian de Laurentis, Shelley Parker, Henry Quesada, Chabad Downtown, The L'chaim Hikers, Erin Downey, and Editor Sarah Moraga. My attorneys, Adam Garson, and Eric Alspaugh.**

A big thank you to all of you who listened to me for hours and encouraged and motivated me through my tears and gallons of coffee. Thanks to **Matt, Tim and Michael** for always listening. Special acknowledgement to all those who kept encouraging me to write and share my stories. Finally, much gratitude to **Bruce, Mike and Nat** for providing mentorship, support, and hope.

Cover Photo: Courtesy of Vladislav Filippov Instagram: @fillvlad
Back photo: Pavel Sfera

Other photos courtesy of Pexel, thank you to:
@Atxroy, @mareefe, Shantanu Pal, Anna Tarazevich, and Vie studio

ABOUT THE AUTHOR

Cindy (Salonista Cynthia) Kosciuczyk earned her early education at St. Mary's Schools in Worcester, MA. She earned her Bachelor of Science in Biochemistry at Worcester Polytechnic Institute, attended Mesa Community College here in San Diego in the Design program, and her Master of Business Administration at University of Phoenix. Her latest training CITI, The Collaborative Institutional Training Initiative (CITI Program) is dedicated to serving the training needs of colleges and universities, healthcare institutions, technology and research organizations, and governmental agencies, as they foster integrity and professional advancement of their learners in collaboration with the NIH.

Taking the road less traveled, her career wove through the threads of science, food, arts, and entertainment. Her work has included hospital research, professional cooking and baking, business administration, media, and technology. She has completed a wide range of training and classes including a Food Manager's License. Her consulting business in the design business, Designer Tastes was established in 2004.

Writing has been Cindy's passion for the past 20 years. She writes for sites in the Persian rug arena, with her latest book published in 2021: Weaving Life (My Magic Carpet Ride through the World of Rugs). Her first book, My Odyssey, was published in 2015. She has been writing and publishing poetry since arriving in San Diego in 2000. A collaborative author in a few books and publications including Biz Catalyst 360, and Beyond the Bridge. Her journey from chemist to chef and back to research put her in contact with many exciting ideas and classes.

Recently Cindy was part of a multi-disciplinary team in a pain Medicine Clinic. She attended the Body Mind College, with nutritional healing in mind. She has worked in an herbal remedy business, a vegetarian restaurant/ supplement business, and has attended many mindfulness and meditation practices including a class with Jon Kabat- Zin way back in Massachusetts, with an instructor from the Esalen Center while overseas, and locally at the Deer Park Monastery.

She currently lives in San Diego, California where she appreciates the weather, great coffee, pets, and early morning writing time. Cindy's optimistic vision for the future is to illuminate our potential for self-healing. Bringing to light for the community a combination of practices that have helped her to be wellness focused rather than illness focused. This program has integrated into living life both luxurious and poetic.

Contact Information
Please contact Cindy at:

E-mail:
cindyk@energi4u.com

Web sites:
www.energi4u.com

www.salonistasays.com

www.designertastes.com

Snail mail:
Cynthia Kosciuczyk
5275 Clairemont Mesa Blvd #7
San Diego, CA 92117

Energi4U Program:
Reach out to me to set up a private consultation:

Cindyk@Energi4u.com

My other books are available from a few different sources including Amazon, my publishers, and through my personal site.

Weaving Life
https://www.google.com/books/edition/Weaving_Life/EHcnEAAAQBAJ?hl=en&kptab=getbook

My Odyssey
https://www.google.com/books/edition/My_Odyssey/HmlvDwAAQBAJ?hl=en

CHARITABLE CONTRIBUTIONS

**Donations can be made to: www.Lupus.org,
www.OptimistInternational.org, or www.vummf.org**

RESOURCES

References

Introduction https://www.visioncenter.org/conditions/iritis/ ref1

Chapter 1

ref2https://journal.crossfit.com/article/coaching-the-mental-side-of-crossfit
ref3https://high5test.com/fixed-mindset/
ref4https://backinmotionsspt.com/motion-is-lotion-why-moving-your-body-is-so-important/
ref5 https://www.everydayhealth.com/autoimmune-disorders/autoimmune-disorders-that-affect-the-blood.aspx
ref 6https://princetonnutrients.com/blog/lower-blood-pressure/
ref 7https://princetonnutrients.com/blog/why-good-blood-circulation-vital-health/
ref 8https://www.merckmanuals.com/home/fundamentals/rehabilitation/physical-therapy-pt
ref 9https://www.deepakchopra.com/

Chapter 2

ref 10https://www.universities.com/find/california/best/healthcare/alternative-medicine
ref 11http://www.lilianllanos.com/emotional-cause-diseases/
ref 12 https://www.wheretotalk.org/news/self-care-through-our-5-senses/#:~:text=We%20can%20work%20on%20one%20sense%20only%20or,look%20at%20it%20without%20describing%20or%20labeling%20it.

Ref 13https://www.thoughtco.com/five-senses-and-how-they-work-3888470
https://www.westonaprice.org/health-topics/modern-foods/senomyx/
Ref 14 https://www.nccih.nih.gov/health/aromatherapy
Ref 15https://www.vitacost.com/blog/list-of-essential-oils-and-their-benefits/
https://web.noom.com/blog/anti-inflammatory-diet/
https://www.scientificamerican.com/article/the-neuroscience-of-changing-your-mind/
Mindset https://www.ncbi.nlm.nih.gov/pmc/articles/PMC5836039/

Chapter 3

https://buddhability.org/practice/what-should-i-see-happen-after-i-start-chanting/
https://www.trappists.org/st-joseph-abbey/
https://yogigo.com/history-of-yoga-timeline/
https://www.eckankar.org/experience/hu-the-sound-of-soul/
https://www.ocf.net/orthodox-music-byzantine-chant/
https://www.myjewishlearning.com/article/the-power-of-hebrew-chant/
https://stayingsharp.aarp.org/about/brain-health/brain-health-and-music-sample/?CMP=KNC-DSO-SSS-NS-June21-BrainHealthAndMusic-5334-Bing-NONMEMBER-MusicTherapy-Exact-NonBrand&&utm_source=bing&utm_medium=cpc&utm_campaign=StayingSharp-NS-June21-NonMember-BrainHealthAndMusic-NonBrand-Exact&utm_term=music%20therapy&utm_content=Music%20Therapy&gclid=a0b53b93cbee16f126205a143f6e5a57&gclsrc=3p.ds
https://bodyharmonypt.com/art-therapy-solution-stress-chronic-pain/#:~:text=Art%20therapy%20as%20a%20solution%20for%20stress%20and,lasting%20longer%20than%203-6%20months%20after%20the%20injury.
https://healthprep.com/topics/living-healthy/10-foods-that-naturally-fight-inflammation/?xcid=663&utm_source=bing&utm_medium=ppc&utm_campaign=370485926&utm_content=1269936647237961&utm_term=best%20foods%20to%20fight%20inflammation&msclkid=2486d87a42ed1bbc8559b9f2f6409eed
https://www.ncbi.nlm.nih.gov/pmc/articles/PMC4572216/
https://www.hopkinsmedicine.org/health/wellness-and-prevention/chinese-medicine?amp=true
https://www.nccih.nih.gov/health/traditional-chinese-medicine-what-you-need-to-know

Chapter 4

https://www.rockitacademy.org/the-importance-of-mentoring/?gclid=CjwKCAiAm7OMBhAQEiwArvGi3JcGndnt9fNSVNNkCsqUURDR0FY9hl2u6lDS98lWigNdlhkGdz3eRhoCescQAvD_BwE
https://www.guider-ai.com/blog/what-is-a-mentor
https://leadonpurposeblog.com/2009/03/13/leaders-are-mentors/#:~:text=%20Leaders%20are%20mentors.%20One%20of%20the%20key,in%2C%20take%20the%20reins%20and%20lead%20more%20effectively

https://ed4career.com/blog/9-types-mentors-have-your-life
https://www.careerexplorer.com/careers/coach/
https://www.henryquesada.com/
https://www.louisehay.com/natural-ways-treat-autoimmune-disease/
https://baptisthealth.net/baptist-health-news/5-benefits-of-having-a-primary-care-physician/
https://pacificucwc.com/
https://www.healthgrades.com/right-care/chronic-pain/pain-medicine-doctor-your-pain-relief-pain-management-specialist
https://entirelyhealth.com/conditions/lupus/main-causes-of-lupus/3/
http://www.moodgym.anu.edu.au/welcome

Chapter 5

https://www.psychologytoday.com/us/blog/here-there-and-everywhere/202001/discover-8-journaling-techniques-better-mental-health?amp
https://positivepsychology.com/benefits-of-journaling/
https://www.self.com/story/how-to-start-a-journaling-practice/amp
https://www.urmc.rochester.edu/encyclopedia/content.aspx?ContentID=4552&ContentTypeID=1
ISBN: **1573229377** ISBN13: **9781573229371Anger: Wisdom for Cooling the Flames** by **Thich Nhat Hanh**
https://www.huffpost.com/entry/things-to-be-grateful-for-list_n_56420d6ce4b0b24aee4bcc63
https://www.health.harvard.edu/healthbeat/giving-thanks-can-make-you-happier
https://www.spring.org.uk/2021/09/gratitude.php

Chapter 6

https://www.mentalhappy.com/blog/heres-how-community-helps-us-heal
https://gritandvirtue.com/3-ways-community-can-catalyze-healing/
https://www.optimist.org/
https://www.healthline.com/health/when-self-care-becomes-community-care#Were-responsible-for-each-other

Product

Robert J. Mendoza
rjmendoz@gmail.com
650-678-3247
Oxidative Stress and Inflammation are #1 Cause of Disease

https://becomingyounger.mynuskin.com

Quizzes

https://advising.unc.edu/wp-content/uploads/sites/341/2020/07/MINDSET-Quiz.pdf
https://www.tryinteract.com/quiz/what-style-of-meditation-is-right-for-you/
https://www.verywellhealth.com/how-autoimmune-diseases-are-treated-5093794
https://www.childrenshospital.org/conditions-and-treatments/conditions/a/autoimmune-diseases/diagnosis
-and-treatment

Illustrations (see attached)

Books:

https://www.amazon.com/Light-Yoga-Revised-B-Iyengar/dp/B000E66B3U

https://www.amazon.com/You-Can-Heal-Your-Life/dp/0937611018

**https://www.amazon.com/Wherever-You-There-Are-Mindfulness/dp/1401307787/ref=sr_1_3?adgrpid=134470
3285359181&hvadid=84044026249167&hvbmt=be&hvdev=c&hvlocphy=164327&hvnetw=o&hvqmt
=e&hvtargid=kwd-84044300265690%3Aloc-190&hydadcr=22560_10768981&keywords=jon+kabat+
zinn+books&qid=1649719750&sr=8-3**

Videos:

Toni Braxton
https://www.youtube.com/watch?v=C0Uv23ELQMQ

Admiral McRaven's Speech
https://www.youtube.com/watch?v=TBuIGBCF9jc&t=6s

Printed in the United States
by Baker & Taylor Publisher Services